Crisis in Masculinity

Leanne Payne

Crossway Books • Wheaton, Illinois
A Division of Good News Publishers

Crisis in Masculinity. *Copyrihgt © 1985 by Leanne Payne. Published by Crossway Books, a division of Good News Publishers, Wheaton, Illinois 60187.*

Fifth printing, 1991

Cover design by Lane Dennis.

Printed in the United Sates of America.

Library of Congress Catalog Card Number 84-72009

ISBN 0-89107-337-X

To the memory of Karl Stern—physician, scientist, philosopher, and great heart—with gratitude for his book The Flight from Woman, which came as an angel of affirmation, assuring me I am not alone in what I have learned and written. It is my hope and prayer that this classic will find its way back into print.

And to another great soul, a woman who has spent her life affirming others, myself included:

Aunt Mary Rhoda Hegberg

Contents

Crisis in Masculinity

Introduction

This book was prompted by my discovery of the great numbers of men who to one degree or another are insecure in their masculinity. In *The Broken Image: Restoring Personal Wholeness Through Healing Prayer* I wrote on the subject of repressed or unaffirmed masculinity as it appears in the homosexual neurosis. But the homosexual neurosis is only one of the ways in which this many-faceted and widespread problem in masculine identity manifests itself. In the present book my aim is to show the problem as it appears in other forms and how those individuals suffering them may be healed in a context of prayer for personal wholeness. That is the chief emphasis of this book, for the need to learn how to pray for this healing is overwhelming, and the positive results of such prayer very great.

In addition, I will point out some of the causes—psychological, historical, and philosophical—of this growing cultural malady, already epidemic in proportions, that I have called the crisis in masculinity. Finally I will examine the nature of the masculine itself, in at least some of its psychological, philosophical, and theological roots. I will, of course, also consider the feminine, for it is impossible to consider one without the other. As is truly recounted in the myth told in Plato's *Symposium,* the masculine and feminine were originally joined together and are ultimately inseparable.

Recently, when speaking to a group on the psychological problem of repressed and unaffirmed masculinity in men, I was interrupted by a woman anxiously waving her hand for permission to be heard. "I don't think anyone knows what masculinity is," she cried out. She is very nearly right. We have come to a time in history when a writer or lecturer needs to explain that to speak of masculine and feminine is not necessarily to speak of the biological characteristics of man and woman. The masculine and the feminine are, in one of their aspects, two complementary poles within each human psyche. By whatever names they are called or understood to be, the masculine and the feminine within man and within woman seek recognition, affirmation, and a proper balance.

Much that is called emotional illness or instability today is merely the masculine or the feminine unaffirmed and out of balance within the personality. *Merely* is always, as C. S. Lewis has said, a dangerous word, and it surely is in this case if one does not recognize the potentially fatal blow an imbalance of the masculine and the feminine can wield, whether to the health of an individual, a society, or an entire civilization. Finally, one needs to add with Karl Stern that sexuality, like "every empirical fact, contains its 'beyond.' " Masculine and feminine have utterly transcendent as well as psychological dimensions. Gender, a vital part of the true self and of personhood, is finally rooted in God.

The case of a man seriously split off from his masculine side and identity was at one time a pathological rarity, a condition to be met with only now and then. Men, affirmed as men by their fathers and the men of the community, were by and large free to mature as husbands, fathers, and leaders. In secure possession of their gender identity, the great majority of men moved from the chest, as it were, out of hearts freed from the legalisms of childhood, the narcissisms of adolescence, or the perfectionisms of an adulthood spent futilely seeking self-acceptance (or even the affirmation of parents). Now, however, what was once the exceptional psychogenic factor has become, unhappily, a ruling feature of the culture at large. Very few men indeed are adequately affirmed *as men* today, and many are pathologically split off from their masculine side altogether.

Though this book is in large part about the healing of men, I want to assure the woman reader that she has not been left out. God created man, male and female, in his image (Gen. 1:26-27). Woman, therefore, even though her sexual and gender identity is gloriously feminine, is man, man with a womb. In this day, individual women often need release from unisex ideas that cloud their gender identity, or even hold them back from accepting and integrating with an unaffirmed feminine side. In such cases, there is a need for getting in touch with the feminine rather than the masculine side (see Judith's story, pp. 123 ff.). Nevertheless, to be whole, not only must her femininity be affirmed, but the masculine within her needs to be recognized, balanced, and, where necessary, strengthened.

The major crisis today, however, is with men. When men are healed, the healing of women will naturally follow. There is an important reason for this. It is the father (or father substitute) who affirms sons and daughters in their sexual identity and therefore—because gender identity is a vital part of personhood itself—*as persons*. Masculinity, as we shall see, is finally not a thing to be learned, but rather a quality to be tasted or experienced. The masculine within is called forth and blessed by the masculine without. It is thereby commissioned to be, to grow, and to mature. Generally speaking, we now have a generation of sons whose fathers, for several generations back, have been unaffirmed as men. The father who is unaffirmed in his own masculinity cannot adequately affirm the son in his.

An automatic and serious consequence of a man's failure to be affirmed in his masculine side is that he will suffer from low self-esteem. He will be unable to accept himself. Men who are unable to fully accept themselves lose to one degree or another the power to act as father, husband, and leader. In short, in at least some part of their personalities they remain immature and become increasingly passive and unable creatively to initiate the changes needed to lift themselves and their families out of the inevitable quagmires of life. The power is within them to do so. The masculine qualities and gifts are there, but they have not been "affirmed" into life.

We are all familiar with the story of Sleeping Beauty and the power of the Prince to bring her to life with a kiss. This is a wonderful picture of the power the father has to affirm the feminine within his daughter, and of the ongoing power of the virile prince in her life to appreciate and affirm the beauty and the giftedness of the feminine.[1]

But in our day we lack the creative images needed to express what happens to a young lad when his father bends over him in love and blesses into life with appropriate word and gesture his inherent masculinity. The quiet tree of masculine strength within the father protects and nurtures the fragile stripling of masculinity within his son. It is chiefly and quite naturally in this way that masculinity is tasted and passed on.

Although a mother's love and affirmation of a son or daughter is important in a thousand ways, she cannot finally tell her son that he is a man, nor her daughter that she is indeed a woman. There are a number of reasons why this is so, and why it is the father (or father substitute) who affirms sons and daughters in their sexual identity and therefore as persons. The most important one is that at puberty and adolescence we are listening for the *masculine voice*. It is the strong, masculine love and affirmation coming through that voice that convinces us that we are truly and finally separate from our mothers. We were born not knowing ourselves as separate from her. If we came to a sense of well-being or of being at all, it was through her love—or that of a good mother substitute. Her eyes, as we nestled in her arms, became the umbilical cord, the life-giving conduit of love through which our sense of being was affirmed, and we began to understand that we were separate and worthy entities in our own right. In other words, we slowly began the arduous task of separating our identity from hers.

The crisis in masculinity consists in the fact that this separation and affirmation of identity is not happening today. We do not come out of puberty and adolescence affirmed as persons. Psychologists have long pointed out that the progression from infancy to maturity involves many steps of psychosocial development, and when we miss one of these we are in trouble. The step of self-acceptance ideally comes just after puberty. The key to taking this step, on the ordinary human level, lies in the love and affirmation of a whole father. Just as the mother is so vital in those first months of life, so is the father in this later period. No matter how whole the mother is psychologically and spiritually, she cannot bridge the gap left by the missing father.

The father need not be literally absent to be missing from the child's life. We're all familiar with the father who is overinvolved in his work and has no time to spend with his children. There are others who, though present, are unloving and remote, or weak and unaffirmed themselves—and so unable to affirm their offspring. One should point out, however, that this rupture between the parents and the child is not always something for which they are responsible. There are many whole fathers or mothers who desire to be present to their teenager, but have lost him or her to a culture that encourages its young to look only to their peers for affirmation and acceptance.

We cannot pass on to the next generation what we do not ourselves possess. Unaffirmed men are unable adequately to affirm their own sons and daughters as male and female and therefore as persons. Until men are once again functioning in this vital capacity, women will continue to attempt to fill the gap in vain, and will continue to verbalize their pain and confusion.

There is, in short, an overwhelming amount of gender confusion in great numbers of men today. When men are healed, the pathway for the wholeness of women will be opened. If, however, men do not begin to find themselves *as men*, the same gender confusion, and on the same scale, will soon cloud the deep mind of women as well.

I begin this book with Richard's story, one of the more complicated and serious cases that illustrate the pain a gifted young man undergoes when he is split off from a vital part of himself. His story also illustrates the incredible joy of tasting a transcendent masculinity, one that puts him in touch with his own.

1 When a Man Walks Alongside Himself

There is a Center in every man in which and through which God works. To that Center He speaks; through that Center He acts. When man discovers his own divine Center, he stands at the gateway to powerful living. (John Gaynor Banks, *The Master and the Disciple*)

"I have never done it before—stepping out of life into the Alongside and looking at oneself living as if one were not alive. Do they all do that in your world, Piebald?" (C. S. Lewis, *Perelandra*)

John, a close friend and associate, phoned just as I sat down to breakfast. His usually cheerful voice was muted by the distress and apprehension he felt over a colleague. The night before he had learned that Richard was in grave need of healing prayer. Richard's problems loomed all the larger in John's eyes because he would never have suspected him of having them. Richard was known professionally as a fine artist whose faith radiated through his art. Socially he was

17

looked to as an exemplary husband, father, and member of his church. As we talked, it was clear from John's urgent tone that Richard needed immediate help and healing.

Opening up to John the night before, Richard had confessed for the first time to a fellow-creature the inhuman and even hellish things that were going on in his life. He told John of dark compulsions that drove him out nightly into the streets of a large city, there to do equally dark, even criminal, deeds. Richard was compulsively addicted to pornography. In addition, while frequenting porn shops he would seek out homosexual encounters. At home his problems centered around his sexual relationship with his wife. Although he loved her dearly, his wife sensed his confused lack of desire for her, while at the same time she felt raped and wounded during their lovemaking. She stoutly resisted his request for mirrors around their bed.

Meanwhile, in his hidden life Richard drank heavily. He would regularly drink to the point of blacking out and vomiting. On a number of such occasions he had criminally exposed himself in public. Once he had even attempted to rape a teenage girl. After narrowly escaping being murdered one night, and on another occasion approaching suicide, he joined Alcoholics Anonymous. Joining A.A. was the first turn for the better in his life, for it enabled him to renounce alcohol. But he realized he was now more than ever in the grip of pornography and homosexuality. As he told me later, "Bigger danger signals than I had ever sensed before began to go off. I knew there was a flaw inside of me, one that had deepened into a crack and then into a gorge, and I knew I could not hold together long."

What this "flaw" was and its tie-in to his addiction to pornography and homosexuality quickly became apparent after Richard arrived for healing prayer. His basic problem was not that he was "bisexual" in the current sense of that term (signifying one who is sexually attracted to, and active with, both men and women), or even that he was "homosexual." Rather, his problem consisted in the fact that he was split off from his masculinity and as a consequence from his real self. In the traditional and best sense of the word *bisexual,* "Man in his fullness is bisexual."[1] That is, man contains within himself at least the vestigial elements of both the masculine and the feminine. The Judaic creation account states that *before* Eve was taken from Adam's body, Adam was created both *male and female* in the image of God (Genesis 1:27). The two, taken together, compose God's image. (The marriage state, in the Judeo-Christian tradition, is a symbolic restitution of this, the bipolar nature of man.) For Richard, the splitting off from his masculinity began, as we shall see, when he was only three years old.

What is it like to be alienated from an important part of oneself—from one's gender identity, with all its powerful archetypal symbols in the deep mind and heart? Psychologically, for Richard to be split off from his masculinity meant he was separated from the power to see and accept himself *as a man.* His inner vision of himself was sadly wanting. Like a gaptoothed grin, his perception of himself held gaping dark spaces. Within his heart there were no pictures of himself as a man and as a person in his own right. Such symbolic, as well as more realistic, images of oneself are taken for granted and are largely unnoticed by the person secure in his gender identity. But inside Richard there was a peculiar void, a nothingness that he attempted to fill with an unhealthy fantasy life. This fantasy life, as well as the images that welled up from his unhealed psyche, provided symbolic pictures of his gender confusion.

There was no way Richard could have lived his life from that Center within him where Christ had been invited to dwell, for he was a man who had long been absent from himself. Rather than moving from that Center, he lived out of the heart of a guilty child under a law he could never measure up to, out of the self-centeredness of an adolescent anxious about every inch of himself, and out of the perfectionism of an artist desperately striving to prove his own value over and over again. His life was split. He truly walked alongside himself.

To one degree or another, countless men share with Richard this painful inner story. One may act it out as a Don Juan, a compulsive seducer of women; another may live as a compulsive liar and boaster in order to prove himself; a third may chronically fear to step out and lead as he is gifted to lead, to speak the truth or act the truth as it is called for. Yet another may simply be caught in the mire of an uncreative, passive loneliness. He will suffer from a sensitive but overly developed feminine side. All, unaffirmed in their masculinity, are trapped in their own failure to accept themselves. All are in turn unable adequately to affirm offspring in their sexual and personal identities.

On that first day I met with Richard he had no understanding of his problem. He only knew himself to be divided within, and that his problems were of the severest kind. Gradually he told me his entire story.

2 Man in Crisis: Richard's Story

"The kingdom of heaven is near." (Matthew 10:7)

Richard's dark eyes looked even larger in his blanched face as I opened the door to greet him on that first visit. Fear of what was in his life as well as what might be ahead for him in the next hour stood out in every inch of his tense features. He soon relaxed, however. And before he began to spill out the things that were burdening his heart, I took his hands in mine and invoked the Presence of our forgiving, holy God.

It is this, the invoking of the Presence, that differentiates prayer for healing of the soul from psychological and other forms of counseling. In this way we are at once more perfectly transported into, and more consciously aware of, the secret kingdom in which we as Christians live and move and find our being. We are in the invisible kingdom, and the King Himself attends His heirs. Richard had come to find his being. He had come that his true self might be freed from the grip his old compulsive false self had upon his actions. My part was to see and call forth into the Presence of the Lord the *real* Richard, and to serve as the instrument through which the Holy Spirit would release that self from its shackles.

As we quieted ourselves in the Presence, I prayed (as I always do) something to this effect: "Lord, thank You for being here. Bring up from Richard's heart and memories precisely those things we need to talk about. And grant to me, Lord, the ears to hear what You are saying, the eyes to see what You are seeing, the mouth to speak what You are speaking. And we thank You in advance, Lord, for the healing and cleansing of Your servant."

In this way the *telling* of the story becomes not only part of its healing but its true *revealing*, for we cannot, without God's help, begin to tell the true tale of our lives. Richard's own words, which he later wrote about our time together, illustrate what can happen when we "listen" to our own story in the Presence of Truth Himself: "I felt as though every time I mentioned another step in the horrible path downward was like throwing a sore or a stone into a deep still pool—behold, they were gone."

The Initial Laying on of Hands

In the Presence, our time together is transformed into an informal but powerful "Office of the Confessional." And because this is so, we don't get sidetracked into paths that lead nowhere. In Richard's case, his need to confess those things at the very top of his conscience was so acute that, before delving far into his story, we started with the confession and forgiveness of those sins of which he was most painfully aware.

In order to calm and bring peace to his mind, I began this prayer with the laying on of hands for the release and healing of his mind—releasing his mind from (and binding) the darkness that had pressed in upon it and had held it in compulsive patterns. We invited the healing light of Christ to flow in and replace that darkness. In this way he was freed to yield up, one by one, those sins and compulsions of which he was most ashamed. In order that his deepest mind and heart might fully participate in this yielding, I asked him to picture with eyes closed Christ on the Cross, dying to take those very sins and sicknesses into Himself. In order that his body also might fully worship and participate in this, assisting his spirit and soul, I asked him to stretch out his hands, palms upward, toward the One he was seeing with the eyes of his heart. This he did gladly, without the least reserve, and we "watched" flow into the body of our Lord each and every dark thing as he named and confessed it. I then proclaimed the full forgiveness of our God and asked the Holy Spirit once again to come in and fill with light all the dark spaces in Richard's soul where these sins and compulsions had been.

Later, writing of this preliminary confession time, Richard expressed what happened in this way: "Leanne prayed with me, and together we came into the Presence of God. I confessed all to Him. . . . He took all of those sins, and He bled over them all and they were gone."

One of the things that came out during this first confession was his deep concern over his sexual relationship with his wife. He told me that he had asked for mirrors around their bed, but that she had not allowed them, and that—though he had been unable to admit this to her—he needed the mirrors in order to function sexually. From this alone I realized how completely Richard was cut off from his masculinity. He admitted, "I have to pretend I'm another man to make love to my wife." Richard need pornographic fantasies in his mind and an image of himself in a mirror in order to perform sexually.

I knew then what we would find in his memories, submerged and otherwise: the story of a young boy split off from and in desperate search of his masculine side. I knew too that these memories would reveal the traumas behind this painful schism from his own gender identity. But before going into prayer for healing of his memories, I asked him to tell me his story, beginning with his childhood. With an occasional question from me, the following picture of his life unfolded.

Richard's History

Richard had grown up in the conservative Midwest, and his father had regularly taken him and his younger brother to a Baptist church and Sunday school. His father was, as Richard put it, "a stern, tough-minded gentleman" of few words who possessed an indefatigable drive to overcome the many obstacles in his path toward even a reasonable financial success. He had once aspired to coach football professionally, but his ambitions were cut short when he eloped with Richard's mother before finishing college. He had then joined a business firm to support the marriage. He was still with that firm and had finally reached executive status, but Richard thought he had paid dearly for that position. For the first ten years of their married life, he and Richard's mother had lived with her parents because they could not afford their own home. Sadly, Richard spoke of his dad's thwarted ambitions: "He never finished school, he never coached, neither of his sons were athletes. My most persistent memory of Dad is of him staring at a game on television, brooding, blowing pipe smoke silently into the air."

Richard's mother came from a family of considerable wealth and social position. Several of her relatives, generations back, had been outstanding artists and politicians. As the college-bound Richard was later to find out, however, all these "famous" family members had failed personally and professionally after receiving money and status. One had ended her life alone, penniless, and an alcoholic after international success as an artist. Others had ended their lives in prescription-drug addiction. According to Richard, his mother had inherited deeply sensitive artistic traits along with the self-destructive nature which accompanied them in her family. With anguish in his voice he told how his mother had lived the life of a wealthy woman without the resources to do so. "She seldom cooked, maids always cleaned, and every Christmas she cried because she didn't have a new mink coat." Over the past ten years she had spent so much time lounging in bed with Valium and high blood pressure that she had gradually become incoherent. She was now unable to drive, write her name, or complete a sentence, and had been diagnosed as mentally diseased.

During Richard's infancy and early youth, his father drank heavily. As the boy grew older, he realized that his father's brooding sense of failure and disappointment over his circumstances in life laid a dark pall over the entire family. In his general negativeness, he never gave any indication of enjoying conjugal intimacy with Richard's mother. He warned his sons to wait as long as possible for marriage because, he said, the thrill lasted only a short while. His earlier drinking seemed to have come out of this disappointment with himself and with his marriage.

Richard remembered one traumatic night when his father, getting out of the family car in a drunken stupor, fell to the ground. His mother, screaming at him to at least consider the children, managed to drag him inside. "My dad looked at me with a horrible sense of shame, and then slunk off into his bedroom while Mother poured out the liquor."

As Richard was dredging up these old memories, he recalled a truly terrible thing that happened to him at the age of four. An older boy had raped him, and he had never been able to tell anyone. Somehow his older brother had found out about it and had run the boy off, but only after the boy had assaulted Richard several times. The rectal penetration had been, in Richard's words, "terrifying and vile."

This memory had stayed repressed until six months before he saw me, when, while he and his wife were giving their little son an enema, it came roaring back into his consciousness. Richard stated that even as a very little boy he had felt "castrated, emasculated, weak, queer, twisted." I took particular note of this memory since homosexual rape, leaving in its wake unresolved and unhealed trauma, a badly wounded self-image, and a monstrous sense of guilt (from participation in the act, albeit unwilling), can and often does open the victim to fears that he is homosexual, and from there can lead into overt homosexuality.[1]

There were other memories rankling in his consciousness that were in equal need of healing, ones that might possibly hold other root traumas behind Richard's later homosexual compulsions. For example, he had memories of his mother, insufficiently clothed and asleep (perhaps drugged) during the daytime, her private parts exposed. He remembered one occasion when he brought in a little friend and shocked him terribly with the sight of his mother, sleeping in the fetal position, her genital area exposed. The Evil One makes use of such incidents as these, especially when they involve a parent, much in the way he uses pornographic material. The shock opens the spiritually immature and unprotected mind to demonic oppression, in the form of temptation and accusation. I knew all these memories would certainly require healing prayer.

It also became very clear, as Richard's story progressed, that his feelings of being "castrated, emasculatd, weak, queer, twisted" were continually strengthed by the father who remained distant and by the mother who, when functioning at all, pampered him in the extreme. To her, he was a helpless, hurting appendage of herself, a self that was narcissistic, depressed, and utterly passive.

Thus, insecure from the first times he could remember, Richard early in grade school began a heroic but unsuccessful struggle to free himself from his mother's sexual identity. He succeeded mainly in forming patterns of striving very hard to achieve what promised (but failed) to satisfy or affirm him as a male. Later on in high school, frantically driven to overachieve in compensation for the flaw or lack he felt in himself, he often studied past midnight in order to get all A's. He joined every club available and was the first to volunteer for the hard jobs. This strenuous effort seemed to please his father; so Richard, the overachiever, grew increasingly competitive.

His adolescence was, in his own words, "disastrous." It was then he discovered that he had little athletic ability. "My father told me that to play football I had to have size and speed and I had neither. I was crushed. I then went out for the church basketball team, and that was a fiasco. After that I threw myself more than ever into studies to try to excel at something. Underneath any success I achieved, though, there was this flaw that I knew was not going to hold under pressure." Richard discovered his artistic talent about this time, and he was praised for it. But neither his talent nor the praise helped him feel better about himself as a man.

In those days Richard had a terrible problem with masturbation—one that had continued with him for some time but in varying degrees of intensity. The fantasies accompanying the habit were even then homosexual in nature. It was the sight of the handsome, athletic male, rather than the attractive female, that stimulated him. The flaw within him began to "deepen into a crack, and then into a gorge." "Outwardly I appeared as a popular, churchgoing, happy A student who had friends and dates. My steady for a year was a beauty queen. [Richard's mother had been a beauty queen.] Everyone knew I had a promising future, but inside all I knew was that I was seeking desperately to feel like a powerful man. I took a body-building course, developed a fine physique, and began to run long distances before school." None of this made Richard feel better about himself as a man. "I never did more than heavy kissing with a date because I was terrified that if she were stimulated to have sex with me, I would be found out as inadequate."

At this point I interrupted the story to explain what I have come to call the "cannibal compulsion," for that was what was at work in Richard's homosexual fantasies. When a man tells me he is experiencing strong desires for another man, I immediately ask him: "What specifically do you admire in this person? Right off the top of your head, what would those things be?" Invariably, in such cases as Richard's, what they admire in the other man will be their own unaffirmed characteristics, those from which they are separated, can in no way see, and therefore cannot accept as part of their own being. These attributes they have projected onto another person.[2]

After such a sufferer states what it is he admires in the other man, I ask him this question: "Do you know why cannibals eat people?" As he shakes his head in the negative, with varying degrees of astonishment, I proceed to tell him what a missionary once told me: "Cannibals eat only those they admire, and they eat them *to get their traits.*" Those who succeed in feigning insanity or some other equally unadmirable trait do not end up in the pot.

In his fantasies Richard was seeing in its idealized form the part of himself from which he was estranged. For him that part lay in what he perceived as the sexual virility of the athletic type. He was looking at others and loving a lost part of himself, a grievously unaffirmed masculinity that he therefore could not recognize and accept. Homosexual activity is often merely the twisted way a person tries to take into himself—in the mistaken way of the cannibal—those attributes of his own personality from which he is estranged. It is actually a form of self-love or narcissism.

Richard had no trouble at all seeing this to be the case in his own life.

At age eighteen, Richard dedicated his life to Christ, and he hoped that this would magically bear away his insecurity, as well as his problems with masturbation. For a couple of years he threw himself so compulsively into Christian student service work that he was simply too tired to feel insecure—or even to masturbate. But then he began to run out of steam. "I feared that I was just distracting myself from my shortcomings instead of facing them. But where does one turn after Christ? When I slowed down from all the activity, I found the homosexual impulses, the desire to molest a woman, the craving for alcohol to ease the spiritual pain. All this was waiting for me like a hideous monster." Aren't I a Christian? Could Christ not overcome these inordinate desires? Richard asked himself such questions continually.

He was to find out, in an amazing experience of God's healing Presence, just how quickly Christ *can* heal such an inner chasm as he had long known. Meanwhile he continued to tell as honestly as he could his agonizing story.

In Richard's last year of college a close Christian friend, who was both athletic and artistic, came to him with wrenching emotional problems. Richard started out to counsel and comfort him, but the night ended in their having sex together. "I didn't know there was despair beyond this, but there would be. We were both so shocked that we didn't think it could possibly happen again, but it did—several times. We finally confessed to some Christians, and their reaction of repulsion gave us the strength to stop."

After this experience Richard reasoned to himself that marriage might be a solution. He thought that perhaps in his Christian work he had just repressed his sexuality, and that it had come barreling out at the first available sexual encounter. Once again, this time while he fell in love with his wife to be, and in anticipation of the "coming solution," he was enabled to leave off masturbating and looking at homosexual and other pornographic pictures.

The next part of his story, that concerning his married life, was the most difficult of all for Richard to tell, because his love and respect for his wife was very great.

"I married a beautiful, charming Christian woman whom I loved and still love. But on our wedding night the divide within me was exposed. When we undressed I was filled with terror and fear of being found out for my lack of normal desire. I immediately fantasized about virile men and managed to perform the sex act successfully." Once again he told me of his search for pornographic material in order to have images to take to bed. "I wanted a mirror in our bedroom so that I could watch us perform and vicariously experience it."

He could not tell his wife that he had to pretend to be another man to make love to her, and his guilt in this regard mushroomed. He could not live with this pretense, one that seemed to him a dastardly deception of his wife. He found that the best cure for the guilt it incurred was a double manhattan. So began a vicious circle: his sense of inadequacy leading to pornography as an aid to sex with his wife, followed by alcohol to relieve the guilt, followed by further guilt over his abuse of alcohol, leading to a greater sense of inadequacy.

In the first years of his marriage, this cycle began to spiral downward. His profession was by its nature highly competitive and unpredictable, and in this too he was desperately seeking to prove himself a man. After several years of struggling to meet its demands, and the birth of a son, Richard began to act out his fantasies outside of marriage. It was then that, fortified with alcohol, he exposed himself and attempted to rape a young girl. He began to drink for days, blacking out and vomiting, and sought homosexual encounters in porno shops. As the cycle moved severely downward, Richard almost lost his life by a murder and then, in utter misery, by his own hand. By this time his marriage was in grave trouble, but he somehow managed to keep his reputation professionally and socially.

After the suicide attempt Richard turned to Alcoholics Anonymous for help and got it. "Joining A.A.," he said, "was like pulling off the Interstate and heading slowly for help after have sped 100 miles an hour with a tire about to come off. There was something about the newfound sobriety and facing of reality which was more bracing and happy than any experience I had yet known." Richard still knew himself to be a man with deep problems, but for a year and a half he was content to categorize them under "alcoholism" because he felt safe while sober. For a while his marriage improved. He even started to enjoy his work. And he began to face his problems—one day at a time.

To be released from alcohol, one must first push through the denial barrier, and this lesson Richard learned well in A.A. He now knew that he had to be brutally honest with himself, and that to run from his other problems would be simply "another form of drunkenness." He therefore gained courage to face his own inner loneliness and to become present to the frightening questions in his heart. Instead of running, he faced them one by one. He began to ask himself many questions. "If alcoholism is basically a physiological disease, was all my drunkenness a sin or a sickness?" "What will I do if homosexuality is a biologically determined trait?"

It was about this time that his mother was diagnosed as mentally diseased, and he asked himself, "Am I doomed to end my life as she and her ancestors did, creative and successful for a time and then finally self-destructive? Is this what it means to be predetermined to hell?" Other of his questions included, "Why do I have so much anxiety about the future?" "Will I ever be able to enjoy people instead of being enslaved to convincing them that I am a success?" "Am I manic-depressive?" "Is A.A. just a good help along the way? Why am I afraid to tell the people in A.A. about my homosexual experience? Why is there no one I can tell my whole story to?"

Richard knew that his sexual problem was not solved, that in fact it was worsening again. He knew also that according to A.A. dogma, alcoholism is considered not a sin but a disease. He feared they would also categorize his homosexuality as a biological problem, and that there would then be no hope for him or for his marriage. Yet he also knew that it was A.A. and not his church that had pulled him back from the brink of total self-destruction. "I did not know where to turn for the answers, but there was a peculiar joy in being able, finally, to ask the questions. I think it was the first stages of confession," Richard later said. "I was no longer drinking myself away from the questions, but I was facing them and prepared to live up to whatever the consequences were."

Richard squarely faced the fact that it had always been male bodies which stimulated him. He faced the fact that his sexual relationship with his wife was, in his words, "a surface illusion," but one he was determined to keep up because he loved her so very much. Therefore, he once again turned to pornographic magazines and movies in order to perform sexually, reasoning that this activity would be comparatively harmless while he remained sober.

The crack within him widened, however, and "bigger danger signals than I had ever sensed before began to go off." His turning once again to pornography was the proverbial straw. Richard began sliding through the crack in his soul, into the hell of a self without God. Unable to reach out and grab anything solid, he knew that he could no longer live a lie; he could no longer deceive his wife. He would have to tell her he could no longer function sexually as a man and that he was incapable of handling the pressures of being head of the household. But he resisted doing so, for Richard loved his family and Christian friends and dreaded the loss of them.

In despair, he reasoned that perhaps God had hated him from the first and had marked him, like Esau, for a personal torment of perversion and brokenness.

Richard Is Finally Able to Tell His Story

At this point of desperation Richard was thrown a lifeline in the form of my friend John. He later called this the beginning of the "mysterious" part of his story:

"I met a Christian brother, and one night we had coffee together. I looked in his face and knew that I could tell him everything I had ever done or felt. It was the first time in my life I had experienced this feeling, and I think it must have been the grace of God. I proceeded to tell him my story. He responded with tremendous love, compassion, patience, and most importantly a sort of divine alarm. . . . His face told me, and he eventually found the words to tell me, that God was going to smash this monster within me and heal me— that it was His Spirit I needed."

John immediately sent him to me for healing prayer. How remarkable, Richard thought, to find himself telling his story once again in the space of a few hours.

We were now ready to pray for the healing of Richard's memories, for his enablement to recognize, accept, and integrate with his masculine side from which he was so grievously estranged, and for the healing of his masculine will. This is not a small prayer; but our God encourages us to pray large ones, those that encompass a life or even the globe on which we live.

The Healing of Memories

The healing of memories is the forgiveness of sin applied at the level of the deep heart (the deep mind, or unconscious)—the level, I must add, for which it was always intended. Agnes Sanford coined the phrase at a time when very little healing was flowing through the church's formal confessional because the central truth of God's forgiveness of sin, along with all the great spiritual realities of the kingdom of God, had been largely relegated to the abstract. Ministers' heads were filled with the psychologies of the day, to the exclusion of an understanding of the power of God which can, and must, flow to the sick and the penitent. This is still most often the case in the ministry, but as Agnes Sanford so clearly states:

> The truth is that any wound to the soul so deep that it is not healed by our own self-searching and prayers is inevitably connected with a subconscious awareness of sin, either our own sins or our grievous reactions to the sins of others.
>
> The therapy that heals these deep wounds could be called the forgiveness of sins or it could be called the healing of memories. Whatever one calls it, there are in many of us wounds so deep that only the mediation of someone else to whom we may "bare our grief" can heal us.[3]

The "mediation" here is not one of analyzing the problem, of empathizing with it, or of attempting to make the person feel better about himself. It is the mediation of the priestly office: that of bringing the healing Christ into the memory, of helping the sufferer to confess his sin or to forgive one who has sinned against him, and of proclaiming (in such a way as the deep heart can receive it) the forgiveness of God.

King David understood this healing very well:

> I acknowledged my sin to you, and my iniquity I did not hide. I said I will confess my transgressions to the

Lord (continually unfolding the past till all is told), then You (instantly) forgave me the guilt and iniquity of my sin. (Psalm 32:5, *Amplified*)

There are three major barriers to the maturity and wholeness of personality to which we are called. The first two, *the failure to forgive others* and *the failure to receive forgiveness for ourselves,* call for what we commonly refer to as the healing of memories. Often these failures have occurred at specific moments in time; hence they are to be found in specific memories. We relive them in prayer, this time with the knowledge that Christ is with us, forgiving us our sins, and enabling us to forgive others who have sinned against us. Sometimes we need enablement to forgive the very circumstances of a long period of time, even a lifetime, that have so deeply wounded us.

Sometimes the memories that need healing go far back, before we can consciously remember anything. After all, why would God heal me of a trauma I can remember and not of one that occurred prenatally, at birth, or in the first months of my life? From experience we know that our Lord not only *can*, but delights in healing those root traumas, no matter at what age in our lives they have occurred.

The failure to accept ourselves is the third big block to inner healing and is actually the main topic of this book. Men who are unaffirmed in their masculinity cannot accept themselves. This block is attitudinal in nature and holds us in various degrees of immaturity. It has to do with diseased attitudinal patterns toward God, the self, and others, ones that are formed in a world where there is not always the love and light required to affirm us as persons. Sometimes the diseased attitudinal patterns are branded into our psyches in the crucible of mental and emotional pain and darkness. Such barriers as these are not leveled instantaneously; for after an initial healing from the Lord, we are then required to take charge over, and change, a lifetime's attitudinal patterns.

Interwoven with these patterns are all the old negative words of self-hatred, bitterness, and unforgiveness—all the lies of the world, the flesh, and the devil that din themselves continuously in our ears until we *deliberately* challenge and refute them. We must then replace them with the healing, life-giving word our Lord is always sending. Here is where the healing of the *will* comes in, for *to listen is to obey.* As we learn to listen to Him, new and harmonious attitudinal patterns are formed, miracle-making ones that lift us above our old mind-set (as well as the mind-set of the age) and enable us as spiritually empowered men and women to take authority over, and break, the negative patterns afflicting our lives and the lives of those who ask for our help.

In short, when we have failed to accept ourselves, a healing and learning process is required that takes a little time.[4] But the healing of memories, the removal of the first two barriers, is an instantaneous thing, even as the psalmist knew. *Instantly* we may be forgiven and released from the guilt and iniquity of our sin.

The Power of the Memory

In prayer for healing of memories, the power of the memory to make the past present to us is extraordinary. The reason for this is that Jesus, the Infinite One who is outside of time and to whom *all times are present,* enters into what for us is a past occurrence, one known only in retrospect, though we experience its consequences in the present. Here the sequence of past, present, and future, in which we experience existence, comes together in a particularly meaningful way with the Eternal. And that which is eternal within us, and therefore not bound by time, is sparked. We experience past and present as one—a foretaste perhaps of a way of knowing earth-time we shall experience when we are no longer bound by space, mass, and time.

George Ritchie, in his book *Return from Tomorrow*, describes a similar experience when he saw all his times on earth telescoped into one. This happened while he was at death's door with double-lobar pneumonia (in fact he was pronounced dead, only to revive later). At this point, as he tells it, he found himself in the presence of Christ:

> When I say He knew everything about me, this was simply an observable fact. For into that room along with His radiant presence—simultaneously, though in telling about it I have to describe them one by one—had also entered every single episode of my entire life. Everything that had ever happened to me was simply there, in full view, contemporary and current, all seemingly taking place at that moment.[5]

Dr. Ritchie—a practicing psychiatrist in the state of Virginia for twenty-seven years—goes on to describe in detail his experience in the Presence of one who loved him beyond his "wildest imagining," of one who knew "every mean, selfish thought and action since the day I was born—and accepted and loved me just the same." Although in the healing of memories incidents return serially, the person will often experience them in detail, with similar intensity.

The Holy Spirit's Action in the Healing of Memories

The essential action, that which differentiates the healing of memories from psychological methodologies, is the action of the Holy Spirit pointing to *the Presence of our Lord who is there*. Our Lord walks, as it were, into the darkest hell of our existence. There, in the unfolding drama of memory, we look with the eyes of our heart and are enabled to see Him. We receive from Him that healing word, glance, or embrace we've needed so long. We forgive others their darkest sins against us, and He forgives us our sins, and then we receive from Him who manifests the very love of God the Father the healing grace we've been unable to receive before. We discover that He was there all along with His healing action, had we only been able to look up and receive it.

Richard's Past

Richard's life had all the classic elements that lead to a repressed masculinity, and, as in his case, to problems with homosexuality as well. His story had yielded more than enough memories which might contain the main trauma and the root of his problem. When we get to the root memory we can, in prayer, pull up the whole diseased plant, including those subsequent traumas that shoot off, like choking tendrils, from the place where the worst things began to happen. It is the place where the rent in the soul began. Sometimes, in cases where the root trauma is deeply repressed, secondary ones leading from it emerge first.[6] But not in Richard's case. When we prayed, asking the Lord to enter into his memories and bring up those needing healing, the first to arise was the root memory, the one when he began to split off from a healthy sense of being and from his masculine side.

The Root Memory in Richard's Past Emerges

The root memory that emerged was a traumatizing fight between his father and his mother, in which the small child Richard stood between them. As the memory-drama unfolded, the mother more or less pushed the little three-year-old at the father saying, "Richard doesn't think you love him." As Richard relived the memory, it became apparent that his mother was angry with his father for drinking and that she was using Richard in order to both shame and manipulate the father into a better behavior. Richard's father reacted to his wife's attempts to manipulate him *by mocking the child*. "I love you," he mocked in the little boy's face as he hugged and kissed him in an angry, grossly exaggerated fashion. Then he yelled, "Is *that* what I'm supposed to do?"

With this and other angry words to his wife, he pushed the rejected child back into the arms of the woman he despised. At that moment Richard totally identified with the feminine presence his father so detested. Utterly traumatized by his father, he split off from his masculine side. The tragedy was compounded by the fact that his father was the masculine presence who ordinarily would have helped him extricate his sexual identity from his mother's femininity (a neurotic femininity at that).

The rest of Richard's story reflects the usual unfortunate consequences that flow, almost as a matter of course, from such an emotional wound as the little three-year-old received that day. This story graphically chronicles his frantic attempts to reintegrate with a true sense of being *and maleness* by winning his father's approbation as a person and as a man.

Seeing Christ in the Memory

As the root memory unfolded, Richard became once again the little three-year-old. It was the little boy within him who was to be healed and set right this day. It was the little three-year-old who would thereafter begin to grow up straight and strong, secure in his own gender identity, and in his own personal identity. So I asked him, as he relived that very moment, to look up and see Jesus with the eyes of his heart right there with him in the midst of his trouble. He was there all along, to heal and to set right; this is what makes the healing of memories so effective. We simply recognize His Presence in the midst of what we had thought to be our own private agony. As the little Richard looked and saw Him there this time, arms outstretched and beckoning to him, he reached out and let our Lord take him from his mother's arms. He felt our Lord hold him close and open his heart wide for the healing it needed. I prayed for him as Christ comforted and healed him in the midst of the memory trauma. I asked that our Lord's own masculine strength would flow into him even in that moment, affirming and strengthening his own. And I gave thanks that this was being done. On his part, Richard vocally forgave his father and mother for their roles in this memory trauma and, continuing to look up into the loving face of Jesus, received from Him strength of *being*.

From there we went quietly into the other memories that branched from this root one, and in each Richard forgave from the depths of his heart and asked forgiveness for his own sins.

The Mystical Marriage

"I in them and you in me . . . let the world know . . ."
(John 17:23)

After prayer for the strengthening and healing of his will (that masculine part of everyone, male or female), I prayed for Richard as he was in the present moment—a man truly ready for the "mystical marriage."

God is so masculine that we are all (men and women alike) feminine in relation to Him. Though certainly true, this is a concept hard for most men to grasp emotionally or experientially. Likewise, it is equally difficult for men to understand the imagery God uses in calling the church His Bride when He invites it into union with Himself. However, what happened in the next prayer with Richard images forth the only true beginning our union with God can have—that of a joyous, obedient union with Christ. I hope Richard's example will help men to better understand the utter beauty and simplicity of the "mystical marriage."

I asked Richard to see our Lord with the eyes of his heart and to *deliberately make his will one with Christ's.*

Then I asked him to picture his own strong male body and, part by part, to make it one with Christ's: his shoulders one with Christ's shoulders, his arms with Christ's arms, his legs with Christ's legs, and so forth. Likewise his eyes, ears, mouth, fingers, and toes—all of them made one with Christ's. As we continued on in this prayer, I then asked Richard simply to invite Christ into himself. Whereas before he had been thinking of and seeing Christ as more or less outside himself, he now saw our Lord walk *inside and become one with himself.* While he was praying with all his heart for Jesus to come in—and actually saw the two of them come together in one—I repeated Jesus' own prayer to the Father: "I in them and you in me . . . let the world know . . ."

This experience illustrates what is meant by incarnational reality, the central and unique truth of Christianity. We waited in the Presence as the incarnational reality of Christ became deeply rooted in Richard, including his imaginative *picture-making faculty.* His conscious and unconscious minds needed to get a firm grasp on this reality and to form a new image of himself in full union with Christ. From this time on, he was to practice the Presence of Christ.

I then prayed for a full release of the Holy Spirit in Richard's life. It is the work of the Holy Spirit to form Christ in us, and He was moving powerfully to do this very thing in Richard. The Christ within needs full freedom (i.e., our full permission) to live His life through us. With the baptism in the Holy Spirit (as this is sometimes called) the giftedness of Christ is released, and our own spirits—fragile containers of God that they are—become strengthened to know, to say, and to do.

As all this was taking place, I prayed that in his union with Christ, Richard would increasingly partake of Jesus' masculinity and would continue to acknowledge, accept, and be affirmed in his own.

It is never possible to express all that happens in a

simple prayer session like this, but Richard's life, within the space of two hours, was utterly changed. Richard later summarized it best in these jubilant words: "I confessed all to Him. I was happy to forgive my father and my mother for their failures to love me. I pleaded forgiveness for my failures to love them. I forgave the boy who raped me and prayed for him too to be made whole. Then the Holy Spirit moved into my person, and from the tip of my toes to the hairs of my head I was cleansed, and then the canyon which was within me slammed back shut. I became whole. I knew my manness and my man-ness knew me."

"I Knew My Man-ness and My Man-ness Knew Me"

Richard was now ready to live from the Center. He would no longer live absent from himself, walking alongside himself. He had experienced what we all may experience: the Presence calling forth the true self out of the hell of the false self. In this resurrection the true self, no longer repressed, fearful, or unsteady, shakes off the pseudo-selves with their myriad faces and comes boldly forward with one face, gathering all that is valid and real in the personality into itself. It is united within. Only then can we realize the freedom to live out from that Center of our being, that place where His Spirit indwells ours and our will is one with His. We begin to practice not only His Presence, but the presence of the new man. We are free from practicing the presence of the old man in whom the principle of sin and death holds sway.

We are also freed from practicing the presence of the immature man who is still under law (see Galatians 4). As Richard well knew, we can be Christians and remain under the law—utterly failing to realize the inheritance of grace which enables us to walk in the Spirit and practice the presence of the new man. Rather, we practice the presence of the guilty little boy or girl, the one still unable to receive the love of God or man, and are rendered unable to exercise mature authority over our own lives or over the body of Christ.

For this reason too, we cannot move strongly and effectively in the healing gifts of the Spirit. False humility, actual sin, or our need for psychological healing keep us from living out from the Center, the position of knowing who we are in Him. This position is one of authority, one in which we, like the unfallen Adam, are *namers* of all that is created. Named by God, and molded by His will alone, we are no longer named and shaped by that which is created. Instead, we move in a maturity and authority that heals the world. We die daily to any selfish or tyrannical authority, any carnal, dominating spirit that comes from living out of the old self-centered man. We also die to that weak position of "no authority," characteristic of the minor under a law. Now we live from the Center, where our Lord dwells, naming in His name. Our true masculinity is restored. All creation is waiting for us to assume our rightful sonship.

Richard left that day exulting in God, his feet (it seemed) hardly touching the ground. But before he left I gave him an assignment that would speed him along in his learning to practice the Presence of God and in learning to listen always to the words God was sending—words that would replace his old negative thought patterns with new and true ones. These would aid him in making a clean hurdle over any barrier to a humble and full acceptance of himself. One day he phoned me after a particularly strong demonic temptation came over him. It came upon him with great force just as he was passing a pornography shop. His newly gained masculinity and authority were thoroughly challenged. But Richard, amazed at the violence of the onslaught, stood practicing the Presence of Christ and utterly put the Tempter to flight. Several other times we talked by phone as Richard asked questions he needed answers to.

Then he came to see me once more, this time for a joyous talk and visit. Several months later he wrote the following:

"Some of the changes which I can share are these: I can experience sexual communion and consummation with my wife with no fantasy or unclean aid. And this is truly a heavenly glory. We almost feel as though we had never made love before, the difference is so drastic from the 'performing' we did while I was broken. It is a sacrament, holy, and a mystery. I almost feel as though it is a little bit of Eden— what we know together as man and wife. Matters of how often or what position seem ludicrous in the presence of this divine act which encompasses and exceeds my deepest desires.

"In my work I can face criticism or misunderstanding. For an artist this is crucial. It was amazing that weeks before I was healed I received a review of my work praising my artistic gifts and abilities, but also acknowledging that I had not seemed to find a center as an artist and that much of my work was 'pushed' on a surface level. Now I have that deep wellspring from which my work comes. I am serving Him in my work—I am secure as a servant pleasing something far greater than I. If someone does not affirm me as an artist, it hurts me, but it does not destroy me—or, more importantly, affect my work. I am rooted in my work and this is joy.

"I can be still or quiet at a festive occasion and be fascinated with the people or the place at hand instead of always having to impress and succeed. I can listen. I can be. I do not have to have another person or another thing affirm me. I even lost any extra weight I had and can stick with pleasure to my goal of training for a fall marathon.

"Before, when I would sin, it was like sinking further in bottomless quicksand. Now, when I fall, I can plant my feet again on something solid and stand once again. His blood continues to cleanse me; his Spirit makes my legs strong to run the race set before me; the Father will receive me with enormous everlasting arms of love.

"My wife and children and friends would echo these praises to the work of God if they were given the chance. . . . I mean it when I say that I am a man, an artist, with a wife and two children, and it is a miracle that I am any of that.

"I still have a 'dramatic' personality, I'm still a sinner, I'm still faced with storms of temptations, and struggles with finances, career, parenthood. But it is as though there is a whole 'place' inside of me now to whom I can retreat and with whom I can overcome . . . anything, even the desire to die. This center, this rock within, is my real self; it is a real, solid-as-gold man."

This is what Richard wrote me, within several months of his healing. Now, a year and a half later, I continue to be amazed as reports come in from all over the country concerning him and his work. Those people who mention him have no idea, of course, of the place from which he has emerged. Just recently one of his fellow-artists said to me, "The light of Christ fairly explodes from that man—what a man of God he is!"

3 Crises in Masculinity Without Sexual Neuroses

Master: The highest masculine impulse is that which "wills My will" for some creative purpose, and holds firmly to that purpose until it is accomplished. . . . Nor will the woman disciple lack a share in these masculine impulses of the soul. She, too, will develop the will to create, to conquer, to overcome; for the redeemed soul must be integrated, "one-d" into that Christ nature in Whom there is ultimately neither male nor female, but One Man in Christ. (John Gaynor Banks, *The Master and the Disciple*)

"I am the way—and the truth and the life. No one comes to the Father except through me. If you really knew me, you would know my Father as well." (John 14:6)

The power to honor the truth—to speak it and *be* it—is at the heart of true masculinity. When a man or woman is stymied in this respect, there is always a crisis in masculinity. Today I heard from a fine, young psychiatrist, one I know to be effective in his chosen field, for we have worked together in the past. But his position on the staff of a prestigious hospital is in jeopardy. As he wrote in his letter, "I just heard the news from my boss that I might not be promoted or asked to stay on because I pray with my private patients!" "Unorthodox treatment" and other such phrases were tossed willy-nilly at him to justify the reprimand.

His boss's mind-set was clearly akin to the one prevailing in Soviet Russia where Christians are given over to mental hospitals for "treatment" of their "disease"—that of being Christian. C. S. Lewis referred to this mind-set in the world of secular healing when he warned a woman:

> Keep clear of psychiatrists unless you know that they are also Christians. Otherwise they start with the assumption that your religion is an illusion and try to "cure" it: and this assumption they make not as professional psychiatrists but as amateur philosophers. Often they have never given the question any serious thought.[1]

This doctor's experience illustrates an important point. He has the courage to be himself even though he has not yet had time to climb the ladder of success in his field. Even though he is a young man, he has been free to honor and live out the truth as he knows it to be. He has not bowed down before the mind-set of the age. Though saddened by his superior's criticism, he has not subjectively reacted to it by thinking of himself as something less than a man. Instead, as these words indicate, he has viewed the situation objectively for what it is: "Christ's presence cannot be experienced unless one steps into the circle of faith. How will an unbelieving scientific community ever be open if it remains outside that circle?" Dr. Tom, undiminished as a person and as a man among men, will go happily to another place where his gifts as a doctor and as a Christian will make room for him.

Two years ago this attitude toward his circumstances would not have been possible. Unaffirmed by his father, he was extremely insecure in his masculinity. He would have been looking to his professional superiors for the affirmation of himself as a man far too much to risk their disapproval. Though suffering from no sexual neurosis, Tom was seeking his masculine identity through success in his profession and would have been unable to risk failure in it. He might even have continued for years, in adolescent fashion, to fear his superiors' authority and power over him. But Tom found healing and affirmation of himself as a man in God, and he was therefore free to be the man God created him to be.

I pray with many men who, finding themselves in the middle of a career trauma, are either paralyzed by it and unable to move in any direction, or are in the process of falling apart inside. Amost invariably their need will be to recognize and integrate with an unaffirmed masculine side. Usually they do not know why they feel so helpless and impotent in their present circumstances, or why on the other hand their reactions to the problem may be so drastic and out of control. Though these men may have no sexual hang-up such as Richard's, they are suffering, as he did, from a crisis in masculinity.

For example, a theologian well-respected in his field came for prayer because he had a writer's block. He simply could not write the essays that were full-blown within him, crying out to be written down. Immediately upon asking the Lord to bring up from his deep heart the reason for this blockage, he became painfully aware of his fear to speak out, his fear of crossing pens with men who held avant-garde theological positions and enjoyed current popularity in his own church and university. As soon as he faced these fears, he began to realize his fear of authority in general and where it had come from. His own father was rigidly authoritarian and impersonal. He could never quite win his approbation. He ached for affirmation of himself as a person and as a man from his male superiors, but he did not really expect to win it. His was a pronounced crisis in masculinity. The true self was stymied, unable to effectively collaborate with the Holy Spirit in giving birth to the essays and books within him.

I have met with academics, professors who found themselves increasingly inhibited in their classrooms and in their scholarly writings because, unaffirmed as men, they were still seeking to prove themselves through success in their professions. Therefore, merely the threat of not getting tenure could hold them back from honoring the truth as they knew and experienced it. Some had conformed for half a lifetime for job security and then wondered why they were depressed and unable to produce. Unfree to live out all God created them to be, they were despairing over lives that constantly missed the mark. They had become lesser men as teachers, as scholars, as truth-bearers than God had given them the capacity to be.

This same story, with variations, is that of the minister who is unable to preach the gospel forcefully because he is inhibited by his vestry, his board of deacons, or even by the recalcitrant men in his congregation. It is that of the husband who from time to time jumps in bed with other women in order to assure himself he is still a man. It is that of the young man who is guilt-ridden over occasional sexual affairs, unable to commit himself to a woman, and now in clinical depression, contemplating suicide.

This same problem is that of the priest or the monk who fears getting alone with God the Father and God the Son, fearful of what the Eternal Masculine will do to him if he draws too close and yields up to Him the deprivations and sin he senses at the base of his soul. His full imagination is therefore fastened on the Virgin, the feminine and maternal, and turned from the One who imparts the masculinity and wholeness he needs.

The man who comes into the Presence and fastens his eyes on the Lord will find not only the Son, but the Father as well. He will find affirmation of his own masculine side. The woman who looks to her Lord will not only be gloriously affirmed in her femininity, but will find that His masculinity, tasted and savored, strengthens her "will to create, to conquer, to overcome." What we look to and see with the eyes of our hearts really matters—the imagery really matters. Whether we are men or women, it is to the Masculine that we must look for the strong, fatherly affirmation of our sexual identity and of ourselves as persons.

I could fill book after book with cases of Christian men who found healing of the severest emotional problems and neuroses by coming into the Presence of God and finding there, in healing prayer, the affirmation of themselves as men. Though their neuroses were not sexual in nature, many of them had been deemed chronic and even hopeless, clinically speaking, and would simply have been treated the rest of their lives for ongoing bouts with depression. But God found the unaffirmed little boy within each one of them and pronounced him a man. He freed them to become the masculine makers he created them to be. Looking back, I can see that the theologians have written their books, the academics have become sacramental channels of scholarly integrity and truth, the priests, ministers, and monks now function as strong leaders, the clinically depressed are joyfully practicing the Presence of God in whom they've found and accepted their higher selves, including the full masculine dimension. There is not time to write of all I have encountered. And they are but the tip of the iceberg, for we live in a time of separation from the masculine, a time in history when the complementarity of masculine and feminine is seriously out of balance.

The following story furnishes an example of how the wounding of the masculine several generations back can affect a family in the present.

The Minister Who Could Not Tell the Truth

Before sharing this story, I would remind the reader that sin is not wiped out by time, but only through repentance and the blood of Jesus. As it turns out, this minister's main problem began two generations before him. The family trauma needed to be faced, and the sin within it confessed, before he could receive the psychological as well as spiritual healing he needed.

The Rev. David B. came for help only after a major part of his congregation had left him, and his wife of twenty years was poised, her suitcase in hand, ready to flee. When I asked him why he had waited so long to get the help he needed (both congregation and wife had been patient and long-suffering), he confessed he had sought help only when he knew he could not live another month without it. He was deeply depressed and definitely suicidal.

The major complaint against him was that he simply could not be trusted to tell the truth. He compulsively exaggerated and often would lie outright. His problem was such that, according to his wife, he would lie and exaggerate even when the exact truth would serve him better.

As it turned out, David was as split off from his masculine side as Richard had been, but the problem did not erupt at the psychological level as a sexual compulsion or neurosis. His compulsive behavior, wild and erratic, was geared toward making money—a great deal of it. He had made and lost several fortunes, all the while running feverishly day and night to secure himself financially. "I have to appear bigger and better than I am. I have to exaggerate so people will like me. I hate myself. There is nothing inside me for others to like. No one could ever love me. I have to make them like me."

Like Richard, David dreaded the prospect of losing the woman he loved and respected: "Most everything I ever did was to try to get her to love me . . . and all the time she did . . . but I couldn't believe it." He also dreaded the thought of losing his Christian family and friends. Filled with the same inner pain that Richard had known, he was a man walking alongside himself, a man living out of a fearful, unhealed, guilty little boy within who could never accept himself or receive the love he so desperately sought from others.

I anticipate that some readers might react strongly here and say, "This man just needs to be born again from above. After all, doesn't Scripture say that he who lies has the Devil for his father?" Others might offer, "He needs the power of God in his life. He needs to be filled with the Spirit." These thoughts might well have been part of my reaction had I not observed this man's heart and his work in the Kingdom—and his long and sorrowful struggle with the chaos in his life. On the one hand, he would pray for the sick in body and see them healed; he would take teams of young people out as evangelists and see the most hardened drug addicts and criminals brought to Christ. On the other hand, he could not spend ten quiet moments alone in prayer. Ministers are supposed to be on their knees a great deal of the time. But when he was still even for a moment, he ran the danger of hearing the accusing voices of self-hatred within. He could not look up and see God with the eyes of his heart; he could see only the specter of an inner nothingness filling the chasm of his being.

Rather than face the enemy within, he put on strong personas: on the one hand that of wheeler-dealer salesman, builder, and businessman; on the other, that of busy minister. Consequently, he never stopped moving. He compulsively involved himself in one frantic activity after another, both to prove himself as a man and to avoid facing the terrible loneliness and pain within. His parishioners, confused by his many faces and finally weary of trying to separate the large amount of good from the bad in their pastor, said to him as they were leaving the church: "We love you, and we see good in you, but we can't take your lying and exaggerating anymore. We have to have a pastor we can look up to."

David's problem was rooted in his past and the past of his family. His family, though Christian in name, was impoverished in nearly every respect. Economically, they were abjectly poor. His father was a sharecropper in North Carolina on land that yielded almost nothing, though the entire family labored long and hard. David received very little formal education and was often pulled out of grade school to work full days in the field. He spent his summers in the South picking cotton alongside other migrant workers, and his earnings were used to buy the seed and other necessities the family needed to exist as sharecroppers year by year. In his family there was, he said, "no time for touching and being touched."

Even if there had been time and energy for it, apparently in this family there was no capacity to touch lovingly. There are families who, though painfully poor, are sustained by a rich spiritual, moral and therefore intellectual heritage. (I am from such a family, my mother having been widowed during the Depression and left with little or no means to support her infants.) But this was not the case in David's family. Though not a great distance from the Atlantic coast, they were separated from the mainstream of American culture by geographical isolation in the hill country, and were closed in by particularly virulent forms of prejudice, ignorance, and suspicion. These things informed their church and religious experience as well as ordinary life. David's father, unable to rise above the local mind-set, and filled with a kind of paranoia toward those who differed from himself, was as a young man harshly authoritarian toward his wife and children. Essentially a good man and well-meaning, he later mellowed. But as a child David had reason to fear him, for his father could be cruel with little provocation. It is not surprising that David left home at age twelve to make his own way in the world, vowing to free himself from the poverty he had known.

As David and I prayed, and as he shared parts of his life he'd never been able to talk about before, I received more and more insight into how the problems of exaggeration and lying had rooted themselves so deeply in his heart and speech. For one thing, he grew up in one of those parts of rural America where hyperbole (exaggeration for effect) is a commonly accepted figure of speech. We see this also in Hebrew poetry, as recorded in the King James Bible. For example:

> I am weary with my groaning; all the night make I my bed to swim; I water my couch with my tears. (Psalm 6:6)

Here we get a true picture of King David's grief, while at the same time we know he did not float off his couch. His use of hyperbole heightens the effect of his poetry and therefore its capacity to convey the depth of his feeling. In no way does it deceive. Pastor David's speech, true to his geographical region, was thick with hyperbole, and it is easy to see how, with his compelling need to "sell" himself, he could stray over the line into falsehood. We talked about this tendency, and for him it was a real eye-opener that the patterns of speech he grew up with lent themselves to his problem.

Problems such as David's have many causes, and deprivation of mother-love in his early life was a large factor in his failure to come to a secure sense of well-being. Yet David early heard his mother lie to his father in order to protect him from a beating. Although she was a woman hard-pressed by life, one who found it difficult to smile or show love openly to her children, she would on these occasions show the love David yearned for by lying to spare him a beating. David thus learned two false lessons from her: it is necessary to lie to survive; lying is a loving act. To unlearn these lessons David would need to invite God into those traumatic memories. He needed to confess his mother's sin of lying and forgive her for its later effects on him. In addition, he needed to forgive her failure to communicate love and his father's ignorant cruelty. When he did, this part of the problem behind his inability to tell the truth was lifted right out of his heart.

We had not yet come to the root cause behind his severe self-hatred, however, and I knew that when we did find it, we would have the problem that had devastated his entire family. David was one of five children, two of whom had committed suicide in their thirties, and one of whom had unsuccessfully tried. Now David himself was suicidal. There was some problem beyond the ordinary holding this family in its grip.

Through hard work and incessant striving, David managed to leave the economic deprivation of his youth behind him. Before achieving this, however, he found the Lord in a deeply meaningful way. His conversion began at age nineteen when he lay dying in a hospital from complications arising from an accident in the factory where he worked. Christians came and prayed for him, and he was miraculously healed. The grace of God was powerful in his life after this time, and David began to witness to others about God's healing power.

When we come to God, He comes into us and sets us free. His new life begins to radiate through us, freeing our feelings, our intellect, our imagination, and our will. Our wills, no longer divided, become one with His. Even our physical bodies are hallowed by His indwelling Presence and are freed to know the cleansing and healing available in Christ. This biblical, incarnational view of man shows us as ultimately free of the limiting world of our own selves and environment; we no longer regard ourselves as hopelessly "determined," irremediably set in certain molds.

In contrast, most secular ideologies view man as determined. The Marxist, for example, sees man as economically determined. Other systems—even religious ones—regard him as determined by environment, biology, sociology, psychology, or by the weight of karma. Although a Christian view of man recognizes the influence of most of these factors, it declares that man is not bound by them, for the gospel has come to set us free. The message of our Lord is, "If the Son sets you free, you will be free indeed" (John 8:36). Why then, since David was a Christian, had he not been freed from all the bonds of his old life?

Although David had most truly come to Christ, because he yet hated himself he could not abide in Christ. To hate oneself is *to walk alongside oneself.* David's life, like Richard's, was split; he was not *one* within. Separated from himself, he could not live and move from that divine Center where Christ dwells. It was not a question of whether he had come to Christ in the first place, or whether he had indeed received the Spirit and His gifts. All of this David had done. Rather, it was a matter of being split psychologically. And this split inevitably affected him spiritually.

Just yesterday I met with a man who, though well-known in Christian ministry, was subject to grievous homosexual falls. Like David and Richard, he was a man who walked alongside himself, living out of the guilty, unaffirmed, rebellious little boy. His case was that of the little boy still battling a baffled mother and stuck in patterns of trying to outwit her. He was geographically far removed from her, but because he had never been able to separate his sexual identity from hers and accept himself as a man, he was still under the law that had chafed him as a child: the law of a mother's rule that, in the absense of a strong, affirming father, is always, and even necessarily, distorted.

"The law revived and I died," said St. Paul (see Romans 7:9, 10). That is always the way it is with the person who walks alongside himself, living out of the immature child still under a law. Our worst compulsions can have a heyday with us when we live in that place, for it is impossible to keep the law. This man, with tears in his eyes, said to me, "But I know the Lord is with me, even when I fall." (He, like Pastor David, had had a dramatic new-birth experience and had later received the laying on of hands for the empowering of the Holy Spirit, with the resulting presence of the gifts of the Holy Spirit in his life.)

The problem here, of course, was that even though the Lord was with him, he stepped outside the Lord, outside the Center where Christ dwells. He failed to *abide* in Christ. When we step outside Him, we step into the abyss, the void, a place where there is no protection. When we withdraw ourselves from obedience, we withdraw ourselves from grace. We are once again "slaves to sin" (Romans 6:16). What the minister was saying to me in effect was this: "Even though I am occasionally a slave to the law of sin, I feel safe in that 'body of death'" (Romans 7:24). According to St. Paul, that is not a safe place to be: "If you live according to the sinful nature, you will die; but if by the Spirit you put to death the misdeeds of the body, you will live" (Romans 8:13).

How safe this man was before he decided to yield up his old immature patterns of rebelling against mother (i.e., before he decided to come out from under her law, accept himself, and live from the Center where Christ had been invited to dwell) can be measured against the safety of anyone yet attempting to keep the law. I personally do not think he was at all safe, and that he was quite far from understanding the freedom we can know as children of God. It is unsafe to hate ourselves, to walk alongside ourselves as immature children or as slaves of sin.

Although each of these men was, in the end, responsible for the ways in which he chose to alleviate his inner pain, each one needed healing prayer in order to become free. Each was in a kind of bondage that he could not escape on his own. Each was like the woman who, crippled by a spirit for eighteen years, was bent over and could not straighten up at all:

> When the Lord saw her, he called her forward and said to her, "Woman, you are set free from your infirmity." Then he put his hands on her, and immediately she straightened up and praised God. (Luke 13:12)

Like this woman's body, the minds of people like Richard and David are gripped and bent down. They cannot straighten up and live victoriously. In healing prayer we loose them from their infirmity: the grip which patterns of self-hatred, rebellion, and lustful or lying fantasies have on their minds. Then, just as the Lord bid the woman stand upright, we say to these dear ones, "You are now free to live from the Center. See that you do it. See that you wait in His Presence until you fully accept yourselves in Him, forsaking the pride that would keep you back from this stance." It is unsafe to walk alongside oneself, to fail to mature, to live out of the unhealed little boy or girl.

Our God eagerly waits to restore to us even the years the cankerworm and the locust have eaten (Joel 2:25). He turns the old wounds, sorrows, and deprivations into healing power. This he longed to do in Pastor David's life. We had only to wait in His Presence for the key, the key that once turned, in prayer, would get at the root cause and help him to overcome his intense self-hatred, accept himself, and stand upright. After a few preliminaries, such as already chronicled, this key quickly appeared. Although he did not recognize it immediately as pertaining to the root problem, I did.

When we begin a prayer for healing of memories, I always ask the Lord to bring up from the deep heart of the needy person *exactly* those things that we need to talk about. Otherwise I do not believe this story would have come up. In it Pastor David told of what recently happened when his brother had taken their aging father ten or so miles from the homestead to visit an ancient Carolina graveyard. Unaccountably, and with no explanation whatsoever, the father had insisted on going to this hidden, out-of-the-way place. The son took the father and was dutifully patient and quiet as the old man searched the overgrown hill that time and man had forgotten. Just as the old man seemed to find the grave he'd been looking for, another old-timer suddenly appeared. And he knew the startled father. He began to gesture with his arms and say, "Oh, I remember that day. I remember that day!" And he went on, paying no attention to David's father who, frantic lest his son hear what the old acquaintance would say, was trying to shush him up. "I remember when the old Indian, your father, was refused burial in the Christian burial ground. I remember when they brought him up here to rest."

Thus came the story—the story of a grandfather whose name and existence had never once been acknowledged to the five grandchildren—a story providing a glimpse of the prejudice, ignorance, and hatred of a community, going back to colonial times. The effects of all this? That was what Pastor David and his brother and sister who were yet alive were still wrestling with—almost three-quarters of a century later. What we do not know can be, at times, the very thing that is killing us.

The family, of course, suffered a terrible sense of rejection due to the racial prejudice of the community. As a child sees itself through the eyes of others, so this family saw and accepted itself according to the community's verdict and estimate. But in the long run it was the family, even more so than the community, who had rejected him. In their attempts to accept themselves and to find acceptance in the very community that rejected their progenitor, they had ended by attempting to wipe the man's very existence from memory.

There is no greater rejection than this: the failure to recognize that a person *is* or has *ever been*.

We have a strange illusion that mere time cancels sins. I have heard others, and I have heard myself, recounting cruelties and falsehoods committed in boyhood as if they were no concern of the present speaker's, and even with laughter. But mere time does nothing either to the fact or to the guilt of sin. The guilt is washed out not by time but by repentance and the blood of Christ.[2]

In some ways it was as if this man's blood yet cried from the ground for justice—for the justice of being recognized for *having been*. One thing was sure: his presence within the very genes of his descendants cried out for recognition. In one sense we cannot cut off any living soul without diminishing ourselves. That is the law of love. We live in and out of one another in far more profound ways than most of us can get a fair understanding of in this life. The poet, with his metaphors ("no man is an island"), gives us occasional glimpses. But we cannot cut off a member of the family, and most especially a father or a mother, without *cutting off a part of ourselves.* In having "hated" their fore-bear, they had hated themselves. This utter rejection of their progenitor was behind the annihilating self-hatred afflicting each member of this family. It was also back of the crisis in masculinity in that family, the reason the men could not accept themselves as men.

> Honor your father and your mother, as the Lord your God has commanded you, so that you may live long and that it may go well with you in the land the Lord your God is giving you. (Deuteronomy 5:16)

The grievous reaction a child has to a parent who deserts, harms, or frustrates it in one way or another often leads to a childhood oath. Time and again I see men in the circumstance of alienation from their masculine side due, at least in part, to a childhood oath or oaths they have made regarding their father:

"I will never, ever love him again."

"I vow never to be like him when I grow up."

"This time he has gone too far. I will never again allow him to get to me."

"He will never get the chance to hurt me again; I'm wiping him out of my world."

For these men to cut off their father by means of this oath was to somehow, in their own psychological depths, cut themselves off from their own masculine side. To reject their father, rather than to forgive him, was to reject and attempt to obliterate him within themselves, a thing they can never stop trying to do. Such is the power of a child-hood oath, and the damage it can do within the psyche. It damages all other relationships as well. After prayer in which these men renounce their childhood vows and extend for-giveness to their fathers, I am often led to pray for God to bless their fathers within their very physical bodies, within their very genes. It's as if in accepting their fathers, they are accepting the part of him that was passed on biologically as well as psychologically. The joy and release this brings is often near to ecstacy. To be separated from a father hurts, no matter how wounded and sinful he may have been, and to reject ourselves in rejecting him certainly compounds the pain.

In David's story we see what a family, cut off from its masculine side, looks like. By "hating" their ancestor, they came to hate themselves. This rejection and denial of their forebear, due to the racial prejudice they had suffered, was behind the self-hatred which overwhelmed the entire family.

In being cut off from the father who is, on the natural level, the affirmer of his sons and daughters both in their gender identity and as persons, they were cut off from the power to accept themselves. The sons could not accept themselves as men. They were a family out of effective touch with the masculine. Therefore, they were unable to initiate the changes needed to pull the family up and out of its deep depression, and into its Center: that place where Christ is always cleansing, healing, and completing.

Confession of the sin (which, as we have seen, time does nothing to efface), along with extension of forgiveness, not only to the community but to the members of the family who chose to forget their Indian grandfather—this is the royal way God has provided for the healing of such a family. That is therefore the way that Pastor David and I prayed. We confessed all the sins, known and unknown, against his grandfather, by the family and by the community. We confessed the sins of prejudice, hatred, unlove, failure to honor parents, and any other sin we could think of, naming it before the Lord. And we thanked God for His forgiveness.

These are "atonement" prayers. It is prayer in which we confess, as accurately as we know how, the sins of a family, people, nations, or given situation. Christ has made the perfect atonement for all sin, and by our confession and repentance of sin, known and unknown, we bring it under the power of His blood. We are not saying that by this prayer the sin of those who lived in the past is forgiven them. What we are saying is that by praying in this way, we break the power of the sins of others in the past or the present over the living.[3]

By repentance and the blood of Christ, then, the way was cleared for the family trauma, with all its evil effects, to be lifted from Pastor David's soul. This prayer action would (and did!) remove the main block that held Pastor David back from the kind of self-acceptance that would in turn enable him to live from the Center. What all else atonement prayers accomplish, I do not know. But I suspect they achieve a very great deal. Other members of the family, even those long since lost to Pastor David's knowledge, would surely find it a great deal easier to enter into wholeness.

I then prayed with David in much the same way as I did with Richard, helping him to see Jesus with the eyes of his heart, helping him to confess all his sin and receive forgiveness for it. I prayed for the *man* within him, that God the Father would find and mightily affirm him *as a man, as a speaker and doer of the truth.* Later he wrote saying, "I'll never forget the day I became *a boy and a man at the same time,* the day Jesus walked back through my life and *affirmed me as a son*" (italics mine). In addition, I helped guide him in listening prayer, that way in which he could exchange his old negative patterns of self-hatred for the healing word that God was always speaking.

A year later he wrote, "I literally ran almost day and night for almost fifty years, trying to find peace. But it never happened till we prayed and I became *somebody.* My whole life has changed. I still have times when I feel I do not deserve this peace. When these times come, I immediately go back to that time in prayer when I became a man and a little boy at the same time. It is wonderful to know I exist for a purpose, and that I am not in the way. After years of frustration, fear, torment, and failure a whole new world is open to me. To know Him, and to *know* that He knows all about me and still loves me, gives me ongoing confidence. He is my confidence, my all. My life has taken on a wholesomeness and integrity that comes only from God. I am having fun at fifty that I missed out on at five."

The extent to which God has and is restoring to this dear man "the years the locusts have eaten" can only be understood in terms of miracle. His wife never ceases to be amazed at the difference in him. "One of the main ways in which this has affected me," she said, "is that *he lets me be myself.*" She and others can now communicate with him. Now that he is listening to God and in touch with his own heart, he can let others be themselves. "After thirty years of being unable to enjoy talking to him, he lets me be a voice without it threatening him. I have a voice with him!" Being from her husband's region, and therefore schooled in the use of colorful hyperbole, she exclaims, "I still almost pass out over it!"

More About Childhood Vows: When a Parent Is Not Easily Honored

A short time ago, while I was sharing with medical professionals the problems which can arise out of childhood oaths, a physician's wife in the audience began to weep bitterly. She had struggled with a nearly total inability to communicate with her husband, her children, or her God. While I spoke, she remembered the strong oath she had made as a child and carried out: a vow never again to speak freely to her father. Unless forced to say a word to him, she did not. This action had made such deep inroads into her psyche that all her later relationships were affected. She literally could not talk freely to those she loved the most. In prayer she renounced this oath and received healing. Her mouth will no longer be stopped by a forgotten childhood vow.

Such prayer is often, as we noted earlier, called for in the case of persons suffering with alienation from their masculine or feminine side. They need help in order to renounce the childhood oath that has cut them off not only from a parent, but from that parent's gender identity within themselves. To fail to fully forgive a parent is to fail to be blessed within our very own spirits, souls, and bodies.

A child can seldom differentiate between its parents as persons and their sinfulness, sickness, or weakness. The parent and the behavior appear to the child to be one. Later, in order to be free, the son or daughter has to separate the two. He has to forgive the sin and accept the sinner. To do this, he or she must gain what I have come to call *the gift of divine objectivity.*

Lacking this gift, the person who needs to renounce a childhood oath will at times be almost scandalized at the thought that such a thing would be asked of him. In a voice filled with amazed injury, anger, or bitterness, he will begin to recite the awful offenses of the parent. And in this recitation we will hear described what it has meant to this person to try to grow up straight under a bent parent: one that is perhaps alcoholic, sexually perverted, mentally unbalanced, cruelly authoritarian, or just plain unloving. Wanting so much the love of the parent, and being unable to get it, is often the greater part of the injury. Indeed, the oath is often uttered as a means to quit reaching out for that love, and so opening oneself to more hurt and disappointment. Renouncing the oath seems to them the same as accepting the behavior, as daring to once again open to the power that parent has to wound and to hurt.

With these persons, new understanding is needed. They must see that they are still subjectively reacting to the circumstances of their youth and, in order to be free, must rise above their subjective stance into an objective one. In other words, they need to rise out of the subjective (immature) position of a child, helplessly flailing in the face of certain parental circumstances, and up into an objective, safe, free position from which they can analyze, name, and accept the situation for what it in truth *is* and *has been*. It is a tough task to face the darkness that is in one's own parents. But through prayer, the obstacles to this facing and naming can be overcome. And it is only in this way that these persons can begin to get their identities separated from both their parents and their past situations, and go on to truly forgive. In this way, too, they can begin to take full responsibility for their own grievous reactions to the problem. They can fully confess and repent of their own sins in the matter.

"But," these persons often object, "I *have* forgiven my father. And I keep on forgiving him." To which I respond, "But you keep expecting him to change (or you are still angry with him for not having changed)" and/or, according to the circumstances, "You keep trying to receive the affirmation from him that he does not have to give." In other words, "You are trying to forgive your parent, but you are not accepting him (or her) as the needy person he in fact is."

I then endeavor to help these dear ones differentiate between the parent and that parent's sickness and sinfulness. Almost invariably they will have thought that to accept the parent *as he is* is to accept the sin and the bentness of that parent. The parent is to be forgiven and *objectively accepted for what he has been and at this moment is,* even while his sin, weakness, and darkness is to be honestly named, confessed, and renounced for what it was and may yet still be. Its effects upon the son or daughter are then to be bound in prayer, and the child is to be set free from any restrictions upon his spirit or soul due to the problem of that parent.

A caution here. A child takes the loss of a parent, whether through death, divorce, or however, as a personal rejection. The rejections we are not healed of we project onto others. In this day when many children are raised in single-parent homes, I often find that a child projects the rejection he has experienced by the loss of a parent onto the parent who has raised him. (It should be noted that this projection is always unconscious.) In a home broken by divorce, for example, the "faithful" parent, the one who did not desert the child, can be scapegoated.

Divorce is a terrible thing, and life can be tough indeed for the youngster growing up in a broken home. I have on a number of occasions watched divorced mothers overcompensate (spoil and make excuses for) their children, and this is due to the false guilt they feel over the divorce. These women had done everything they knew to keep their homes together, but had failed due to gross immaturity, narcissism, or some such thing on the part of the husband. Feeling guilt over their failure to succeed in marriage, almost invariably these mothers overcompensated their children, and their children perceived the false guilt as real guilt.

In this way, and I'm sure there are others, we can see how children's perceptions are often awry. I always wince when I hear a child has written an exposé type of "life story" of a parent. What they see as "fact" may be very real psychological projections. At any rate, when we pray for the objectivity that is needed, these projections come to light. It is not at all unusual to find a son or daughter, as they begin to forgive, begin at the same time to realize that some of their grievances against a parent are unfounded, that it is in fact necessary to forgive the *other* parent, the idealized one whose absence they have unconsciously taken as a personal rejection.

"Honor your father and your mother, as the Lord your God has commanded you, so that you may live long and that it may go well with you in the land the Lord your God is giving you. (Deuteronomy 5:16)

How is this done when a parent is truly perverse? Actually, as we have already indicated, we can obey our God in this difficult matter (prayer makes all the difference), and to do so is truly to find life. We must find that *divine objectivity* which allows us to love and wisely pity that unhealed soul close to us, while at the same time we avoid being overly diminished by the darkness, inability to love, or whatever is amiss within that soul. Within this objectivity must be built the understanding that "love is something more stern and splendid then mere kindness" (C. S. Lewis), that this love knows nothing of unwisely putting oneself back under the power of whatever darkness grips another soul. That sort of "love" or "submission" helps no one.

A prayer such as the following can enable one to honor and accept a parent not easily honored, and from there one can go on to renounce any childhood oaths concerning such a parent or circumstance:

"Father, I thank You for creating my father (or my mother) in Your image. With all my heart I forgive him for not becoming all You created him to be. I realize now that he needed the healing that I am even now receiving. Some way, somehow, Lord, as I accept and forgive my father, may his life as it has been handed on to me become all You ever intended it to be. Lord, I do forgive him all his offenses against me. I do accept him *as he is,* an unhealed and needy person. There but for Your grace, I would be. I thank You for all You made him to be, all You created him to be. I will look for the real person You intended him to be, and in Your Name I will affirm it whenever I see it. I look to You now, for the affirmation I always wanted so badly from him. Love him when You can, Lord, through me."

And I go on to pray in such a way as the heart of the child can see itself no longer subjectively reacting to the parent, but calmly reaching out to him a hand of blessing *if and when* the opportunity presents itself. (He is to be in no hurry to test out his ability to "bless," as time is required for the son or daughter to grow in their newfound objectivity— time in which their emotional reactions to the parent are changed, and the old subjective patterns give way to healthier, more secure ones.) In this way, the son or daughter can begin to see himself as the "blesser," and is no longer to agonize over the fact that the parent is unable to bless him (or even reform) in return.

The way is then open for the son or daughter to accept himself. He has been blocked in this heretofore, at least in part, because he has been unable to accept his progenitor. He therefore cannot like or accept himself. "Am I not bone of their bone, flesh of their flesh?" he thinks, and when he looks in the mirror he sees them. To hate a parent is, in the end, to hate oneself.

After prayers for enablement to accept a parent, I am often led to lay hands on the son or daughter and to pray for the father or mother as he or she has been inherited (genetically, biologically, psychologically, or however) within the very cells of the son or daughter's being. This is always an exciting and joyful prayer, the moment when the child acknowledges and receives the blessing of God upon the part of himself inherited from the previously "unacceptable" parent. Remarkable blessing comes out of this way of prayer, and real acceptance takes place.

I prayed for God to bless the Indian within Pastor David, and it was as if he integrated with a long lost part of himself. Multitudes of black people in the United States, and especially black men, need the very type of illumination, prayer, and healing that Pastor David received. The crisis in masculinity among blacks in our country can and must be healed. May it be so, and soon. Needless to say, Indians, blacks, Jews, and others who have experienced great rejection due to race have special needs in the area of healing of memories.

The following story illustrates how difficult it can sometimes be to accept a parent as he or she is, and it also reveals the ongoing battle with the failure to accept oneself when this divine objectivity is not achieved.

The Doctor Who Hated His Face in the Mirror

A Christian physician, loved by everyone who knows him, had a most difficult time in accepting himself fully. Every morning, as he shaved, he was reminded of this need because he did not like to see his own face in the mirror. He is a man wonderfully used of God, and therefore one who has prayed continuously for the grace to overcome the problem of self-hatred—if for no other reason than in order to accept the vocation God has given him. Anointed by God to pray for the sick, he has *had* to live from the Center, at least part of the time. But he knows the danger of running from God's perfect will for himself when, judging himself unacceptable, he steps alongside and looks at himself with excessive distrust and unlove.

As he grew in the favor and admiration of others, and in success both as a physician and as a Christian serving in the public eye, his self-hatred pained him all the more. All kinds of new fears about himself set in: "Why do I seek out friendships with good-looking, handsome, athletic men?" Before his involvement in Christian ministry, he had kept his feelings, fears, yearnings, needs, and loneliness to himself. In fact, before his experience of renewal in the Spirit he had kept a stern authoritarian control over both himself and his family, a control that kept true conversation with them at a safe distance. Rarely, therefore, could he share meaningfully even with his wife. To do so might mean to look, even for a moment, at his fears, and then he would have to believe the worst of himself. But gradually, as he came present to the Lord, he came present to his own heart and gained the courage to look at his feelings and fears. After hearing me speak and reading *The Broken Image,* he realized and faced the fact that although he did not have a sexual neurosis, he was severely cut off from his masculine side. He simply could not accept himself as a man.

He came to talk to me about his fears, the main one being, "Why am I so desperate for male companionship? Is there really something wrong with me? I have never looked at myself as being masculine; by that I mean 'handsome, rugged, athletic.' I see myself as being different, odd, seeking male approval and companionship. I like to be creative, do gardening, read, travel, dress well, and I am 'people-oriented,' I'm a 'hugger.' And I feel I must apologize for being this way, that I must try to hide my creativity and my gifts."

As we talked, his agitation concerning his father quickly became apparent: "I have never felt loved or affirmed as a son or as a man by my father. I don't ever remember him holding me, telling me he loves me, that I am good, or that he is proud of me."

If ever a man needed to be lifted from the subjective to the objective position where his father was concerned, this good man did. He still yearned for his dad's love and affirmation; he still grew angry with him for not giving it. He looked for his father to change, and he went through all the gamut of emotions over and over again as he reached out to his father and as his father remained precisely the man he had always been: unloving, unreasonable, and always accusing others of neglecting him. At my suggestion that he, the physician, must gain the objectivity to see and accept his father as he in fact was, and that we would pray to this end, the pitch of his voice must have rose an octave: "But you don't know what you are asking! We can't accept him *that* way."

And out came the picture of what it had meant to try

to grow up straight in the midst of an evil perversity. His father, a rich man, was also a miser. Although he owned thousands of acres of rich orchards in Oregon, he never gave anything to his wife or children that cost him anything—whether in the way of loving actions or even the lowliest gift. One of the doctor's most agonizing charges against his father was, "He never once gave me a gift. He is a rich man, and for my birthday he gives me coupons that cost him nothing." Throughout his school and college years the son had spent vacations laboring in the father's orchards. Although he was well-paid, he had no sense of partnership with his father in this enterprise. His father remained as aloof toward him as toward the other workers. Through his work he came to know the magnitude of his father's holdings and remarked to me in bitterness, "My mother died without having even the most common laborsaving devices or a penny to jangle in her pockets. He even did the grocery shopping."

As he shared about his father's words and actions toward himself, I saw him as a miracle sitting before me. A "miracle," true enough, who was not yet affirmed in his masculine identity or as a person, and one who had yet to gain the objectivity needed to creatively handle the problem with his father. But few sons survive such a negation of themselves as this father was able to dish out. A man who negated life and love, this father had failed to snuff out the essential spirit, the *life* in his son. It was almost as if he had tried, albeit unconsciously. He had wounded him dreadfully, and if God had not helped this son, that son could have (by hating or failing to forgive his father) become a little more like him every year.

This is the problem with the childhood oath, with the childhood determination to "never be like my father." Apart from accepting and forgiving our parents, *as they are,* we cannot get our identities separated from them and go on to accept ourselves. We are therefore in danger of becoming more and more like them. To fully forgive is divine, and divine intervention is required to do it. "Yes," said the doctor to this insight, "before I found Christ in a deeply meaningful way and began the work of forgiving, I was becoming more like him every year."

Nevertheless, the work of forgiveness to be done was not finished in Dr. L.'s life. He was now face to face with his need to receive the gift of divine objectivity, to be raised from the subjective little-boy position in relationship to his father to one of adult maturity with its capacity to stand above a problem, see it for what it is, name it before God, utterly forgive it, and no longer be grievously entangled in it. It's one thing to suffer a problem while looking down upon it from a free perch, and quite another to suffer it while still having one's feet, like a captive bird, caught in the net. For Dr. L. to achieve the objective position, he must now accept his father as the man he in fact is and always has been. After explaining to him his need, I helped him to pray in the following fashion:

"I forgive you, Dad, for being unable to love me, unable to give to me or to my mother, my brother, and my sister. I face the illness and wickedness of your particular brand of miserliness, and I name it as the evil it is, as an evil with the power to wound my mother and my sister (even fatally perhaps, for they both died early of physical diseases), and myself. That you could never see or treat us as *persons*, that you could not affirm the life that was given us, but could only see everything in terms of your own small and even perverted desires, I forgive you. I forgive you for not becoming all God created you to be, I accept you as you have chosen to be, and I will no longer strive uselessly, demanding that you change, demanding that you love me, that you recognize me as a person with needs, feelings, aspirations, and desires. But because I can now truly forgive you, I will no longer give you the power to wound me or my own wife and children. We name the evil, and in the Name of Him who is our light and life, we surmount it, we transcend it in the power of the Spirit. We can now bless you as you let us, expecting nothing in return. We do not accept your attempts to scapegoat us, but with the word of truth, that wisdom that comes from God, we turn your accusations and projections back upon your own head, and we leave you to deal with them. We know now that this is love, the love that 'is more stern and splendid than mere kindness.' It is the love, this word of truth, that will help you overcome the evil that binds you to yourself. We do not judge you, Dad, but we do judge the evil that has wounded us all.

"And now, Heavenly Father, I thank You for hearing this prayer, for enabling me to accept and fully forgive my father, and for enabling me to no longer subjectively flail under the evil that has afflicted us all, but to rise into that true objectivity that will perhaps someday enable me to be a channel of Your healing love to my father."

In this way, Dr. L came into that green and spacious place where he began to know God the Father's affirmation of himself as a son and as a man. He began to hear the voice of the ultimate Affirmer. "On my first eight-day retreat, I heard the Father tell me He loved me, that I was precious in His eyes, and that He needed me to do His work. This permeated my entire being. . . . 'I love you and now call your sexuality [masculinity] into order so that you can grow in My love and then minister to men I call you to.'"

In this way, listening to the affirming words of God the Father, he began to "bond" with Him; he made contact with ultimate masculinity, which in turn struck fire to his own. And he began to gain, slowly at first, the gift of divine objectivity.

Dr. L could now see that his deep desire for male relationships, never a bad thing in itself but rather needful and healthy for all men, was frightening to him because he had 1) a fear of rejection by other men, and 2) such an overwhelming need for their affirmation of himself as a man. He had never bonded with his father and unconsciously sought this masculine bonding through other men. His need for masculine approval and love had been so great, therefore, that he had had to repress it, and rankling as it did, deep in his unconscious, it began to erupt as fear, guilt, odd thoughts, genital responses, impotency with his wife, and finally, as time went on, to an unhealthy fantasy life in order to perform sexually.

As Dr. L. came present to and understood his own heart, all repression of his need for father-love and masculine approval stopped. Then once it moved into the conscious mind where it could be laid before the Lord, it could no longer erupt in odd ways. He repented of and put to death the fantasy life he had adopted in response to his fears and guilt; his problems with impotency, inappropriate genital responses, and odd thoughts subsided and disappeared.

From then on he could begin to relate to men. He was no longer afraid to put his arms around the man who needed his touch, hold him tight, and pray with him—whether this was in his capacity as a physician treating the ill and diseased, or as a layman called to pray with and for others. Dr. L. had a medical practice in a large West Coast port. His large medical practice brought him all conditions of men and women. As a specialist in his medical field, he is often called upon to treat medical problems that are specific to practicing homosexual males. Before his healing, these patients could bring to life the worst fears he had about himself. Now, however, in his own words, "I can talk with, pray with, cry with" the homosexual person. "I have become more lovingly authoritative or firm in speaking about sexual behavior to the men who come to me." Dr. L. now has, in fact, a most significant ministry to men suffering with sexual neuroses and, because of the cosmopolitan nature of his city, has helped people from many lands.

As infants snuggling in our mother's arms, sons and daughters alike are affirmed in their feminine side. We get in close touch with the feminine within our mothers and therefore within ourselves. Dr. L., having had a loving, understanding mother, was highly developed in his feminine side. And this was a very good thing indeed. But, being insecure in his masculine side, he had been fearful and ashamed of his giftedness. He had even tried to hide the creativity that came directly out of being in close touch with his intuitive, feeling, compassionate self.

"As Leanne and I prayed about masculinity/femininity and their balance, I began to see myself differently. I began to see myself in the light of Jesus. I also saw the balance within Jesus; His masculinity/femininity became more obvious, and His relationships with both men and women."

As this physician understood this, he recognized and accepted his own unique gifts.

One young man, suffering a full-blown homosexual neurosis, told me that his father had never once, even though he lived in the home, entered his bedroom. He told me that he could not remember his father ever intentionally touching him. Understandably, this son had as a child an overwhelming need to touch his father. To touch the father, the ordained role model from whom masculinity is received, is a basic need for a son. To have never grasped hands with a father, roughhoused with him, rubbed shoulders with him in a physical way, especially when he lives within touching distance, can be a deprivation beyond what most people can imagine. If this father had been present to his son in the many other ways that count, his deprivation would, of course, have been ameliorated.

This young man, like Dr. L., had never bonded with his father; the masculine within him had never had the opportunity of "striking" the masculine within another in such a way as to allow it to flame into life. His deprivation of father-love, father-touch, father-communication later erupted in compulsions to touch and be touched by other men. His guilt over this led him to believe he was homosexual, and from there he got into the lifestyle. The lifestyle does not heal the deprivation, so very difficult to be made up for in later years. He was healed, even as Dr. L. was, by coming into and bonding with God the Father. Only He can heal the human person of such an unnatural deprivation as this young man knew. Only He could have brought Dr. L. or this other young man into the extraordinary joy and wholeness they now know.

Men, in order to know themselves as men, need to touch, firmly and appropriately, other men. "As iron sharpens iron, so one man sharpens another" (Proverbs 27:17). In an earlier book I wrote,

> Because heaven and earth are crammed with living creatures and concrete things, awesome to know in their reality, man is only becoming whole while reaching out to them, i.e., when he is outer-directed. He can only know himself by knowing others, by coming to taste, in a manner of speaking, the incredible variety of *isness* that resides outside himself.[4]

This is an especially significant principle in regard to gender identity. The masculine within the male *knows and becomes conscious of itself* as it is enabled to see and touch the reality in another male. When a young man is fortunate enough to grow up with a father whose masculinity, in its transcendent as well as biological and psychological dimensions, are intact and affirmed, he has the opportunity to experience and integrate with his own masculine side. Spiritually, psychologically, and physically, he will be outer-directed and therefore sharpened, deepened, and broadened by all that *is* as he connects with and participates in the awesome realities outside himself.

4　What Is Masculinity?

"Yes," said the Director. "There is no escape. If it were a virginal rejection of the male, He would allow it. Such souls can bypass the male and go on to meet something far more masculine, higher up, to which they must make yet a deeper surrender. . . . The male you could have escaped, for it exists only on the biological level. But the masculine none of us can escape. What is above and beyond all things is so masculine that we are all feminine in relation to it. You had better agree with your adversary quickly."

"You mean I shall have to become a Christian?" said Jane.

"It looks like it," said the Director. (C. S. Lewis, *That Hideous Strength*)

[T]he deepest search in life, it seemed to me, the thing that in one way or another was central to all living was man's search to find a father, not merely the father of his flesh, not merely the lost father of his youth, but the image of a strength and wisdom external to his need and superior to his hunger, to which the belief and power of his own life could be united. (Thomas Wolfe, "The Story of a Novel," in *The Creative Process: A Symposium*)

The Transcendent Nature of Gender

Earlier in this century Karl Stern found it necessary to remind his readers that sexuality and in fact "every empirical fact contains its 'beyond.' "[1] C. S. Lewis also found it necessary to explain that to speak of masculine and feminine is not necessarily to speak of the biological characteristics of man and woman. Lewis perhaps brought this fact home to the minds of his readers most effectively in two novels, *Perelandra* and *That Hideous Strength*. In the mouth of his protagonist, Ransom, we read some of Lewis's finest assertions on the subject:

> "Gender is a reality and a more fundamental reality than sex. Sex is, in fact, merely the adaptation to organic life of a fundamental polarity which divides all created beings. Female sex is simply one of the things which has feminine gender; there are many others and Masculine and Feminine meet us on planes of reality where male and female would be simply meaningless. . . . The male and female of organic creatures are rather faint and blurred reflections of masculine and feminine. . . . Their reproductive functions, their differences in shape and size partly exhibit, partly also confuse and mis-represent, the real polarity."[2]

To think on the transcendent nature of gender is awe-inspiring, for sexuality and gender are grounded in the Being of God and His creation. Masculinity and femininity, rooted in God, have utterly transcendent dimensions.

God as Masculine and Feminine

Thou wilt keep him in perfect peace whose imagination is stayed on thee. (Isaiah 26:3, R.V., margin)

"Image and apprehension cleave . . . together,"[3] and in the imagery of biblical revelation God has taught us to see and worship Him as the Father who loves us, molds us, and seeks communion. "The Lord your God loves you" (Deuteronomy 23:5). "If you, then, though you are evil, know how to give good gifts to your children, how much more will your Father in heaven give good gifts to those who ask him!" (Matthew 7:11). "Yet, O Lord, you are our Father. We are the clay, you are the potter; we are all the work of your hand" (Isaiah 64:8). "A father to the fatherless, a defender of widows, is God in his holy dwelling" (Psalm 68:5). "This is how you should pray, 'Our Father in heaven, hallowed be your name' " (Matthew 6:9). Throughout both the Old and New Testaments, God is presented to us as Father.

But also, through the biblical imagery, we see that God loves us as a mother: "As a mother comforts her child, so will I comfort you" (Isaiah 66:13). "O Jerusalem, Jerusalem, you who kill the prophets and stone those sent to you, how often I have longed to gather your children together, as a hen gathers her chicks under her wings, but you were not willing!" (Luke 13:34).

After this chapter was mostly finished and ready for editing, several of my prayer partners laid hands on me and prayed that I would find the additional words and images I needed in order to speak more clearly of the transcendent nature of gender. The transcendent nature of anything is not, in our materialistic age, an easy subject to write about, and most especially that of gender and sexuality. And since this chapter was to be specifically on the transcendent nature of masculinity, we asked especially for help with that. When we turn the eyes of our hearts up to the Father for guidance, He is as apt to send us a picture or a vision (when we are open to receive it) as an impression, thought, or word. Immediately a vision came to one of us, and in the words of the prayer partner who received the following vision: "It was of God as 'Mother,' pregnant with creativity, ready to give birth. It seemed this vision related to the prayer group. The creativity within the womb of the being in the vision was electric with energy, ready to burst forward, seemingly to affect the universal scene of God's handiwork. It was the 'mother' in God—mothering his flock—ready to breathe upon us as in the beginning of all creation." This was a feminine image to say the least, and my prayer partner was much taken aback. Quickly she had us pray for discernment. Looking to God as Father, she had seen Him as Mother.

Yet this vision was most certainly from God. He was speaking powerfully to us of Himself, a God in whom all real good is contained, the feminine as well as the masculine. I thought of the picture of Christ I had had only a few days before when, terribly weary, I had looked to Him in prayer. I had faced terrible evil, having been involved in freeing a number of people who were grievously beset by demons through occult activity. Drained to the dregs, as it were, the vital forces within me were in great need of God's renewing touch. As I looked to Jesus for this renewing, I "saw" with the eyes of my heart Christ's strong masculine breast and shoulder: bare, tanned, vital with physical human strength, much as it must have been when he brooded over Jerusalem and said: "How often I have longed to gather your children together, as a hen gathers her chicks under her wings, but you were not willing" (Matthew 23:37). As I prayed, the picture of the virile, masculine breast and shoulder remained, and I leaned my head upon His breast and was strengthened and renewed, *as by a mother.* It was as if I were a little child, rocked in the arms of Christ, at once God the Son and a mothering, nurturing, healing God.

In both these instances we see the appropriateness of these images as they pertain to God. The images are both masculine and feminine because ultimate masculinity and ultimate femininity are rooted in Him. God is truth. The God who is pregnant with all that is *real,* out of whose uncreated womb all *creating* is birthed, He is the One so masculine that we all, men and women alike, are feminine in relation to Him. Nevertheless, because God holds all real good within Himself, the images we have of Him will contain both the masculine and the feminine.

The true or the higher self in each one of us is the essential self in union with God. It partakes richly of Him. In relation to God, this self (whether the man-soul or the woman-soul) has always been understood to be feminine. "What is above and beyond all things is so masculine that we are all feminine in relation to it." We are, therefore, as Lewis points out, "dealing with male and female, not merely as facts of nature, but as the live and awful shadows of realities utterly beyond our control and largely beyond our *direct knowledge,* or rather, we are not dealing with them but (as we shall soon learn if we meddle) they are dealing with us."[4]

The polarity of the sexes, for example, and their union in marriage corresponds to, and is analogous to, the union between God and man. Lewis says it this way: "One of the ends for which sex was created was to symbolize to us the hidden things of God. One of the functions of human marriage is to express the nature of the union between Christ and the Church."[5] Insofar as we are the receivers and God is the initiator in our relationship to Him, the predominance of the image of God as masculine is symbolically accurate.

On the level of Nature, as male and female biologically, we are representative of the great cosmic masculine and feminine dualities. We are the indispensable polar entities that in union help make possible the Great Dance of all created things:

> In the act of love we are not merely ourselves. We are also representatives. It is here no impoverishment but an enrichment to be aware that forces older and less personal than we work through us. In us all the masculinity and femininity of the world, all that is assailant and responsive, are momentarily focused. The man does play the Sky-Father and the woman the Earth-Mother; he does play Form, and she Matter.[6]

On yet another level, the polarity of the sexes corresponds to a polarity in the human ways of *knowing,* that of the masculine discursive reason and of the feminine intuitive mind. It takes *form* (the power of the masculine analytical intelligence to thrust forward and give matter its objective form) in union with *matter* (the feminine intuitive mind fraught with *meaning)* to not only yield but preserve the good of reason and knowing.

Form has been separated from matter; the masculine mind has split off from the feminine mind in our ways of knowing. Our ways of knowing should include intuition, or *direct knowledge,* which complements empirical or scientific knowledge, the only knowledge that modern man for all practical purposes acknowledges.[7] It should also reflect the good of reason, but due to the divorce between the masculine and feminine minds, a perverse and materialistic rationalism has usurped the place of reason, which balances and combines the analytical and the intuitive. Men everywhere are separated from their own hearts, the "feminine" within them and within their female counterparts, and are therefore unable to get in touch with the mystery of *being.*

Because form is separated from matter in our ways of

knowing, the masculine scientific mind divorced from the feminine intuitive mind, man sees himself as primarily a biological creature and has formulated a biological and chemical view of himself and even of his own mind. This leaves no room for mystery, for awe and humility at the prospect of getting in touch with the transcendent dimensions of one's male-ness, one's female-ness, one's real and higher self in God.

"I knew my man-ness and my man-ness knew me," is what Richard wrote some months after the Lord cleansed and healed him. Richard's "man-ness" was a quality he began to experience as, with God's help, he got in touch with and accepted the masculine self. This was not a reality he could have received through the masculine ways of knowing—that is, through logical speculation or study about it. He could never have gotten in touch with transcendent truth through scientific or cognitive means. We can never find such truth in a test tube. Nor can we find it by debating such issues in college classrooms, feminist forums, courts of law, or even in ecclesiastical courts. Masculinity—along with all that partakes of the unseen real—is to be tasted. It is apprehended and known, like all our knowledge of spiritual reality, by an experience of the heart—the heart's way of knowing. This can be termed the true imagination—the heart's capacity to *intuit* the unseen real, and even to *conceive* it, as in the conception of a child by a woman.

The difference is that of being *in* an experience as opposed to studying *about* it. A man, for example, cannot kiss his sweetheart and analyze that kiss at the same time. Two different kinds of knowing are here involved, the heart's and the head's. To persist in attempts to analyze experience while *in it* is to destroy experience, to fracture and fragment the heart's way of knowing. To habitually do this leads to what I have come to call "the disease of introspection," that dreadful and prevalent modern condition whereby a person loses the capacity to *be,* to experience life and love firsthand. Such a one can truly be said to "walk alongside himself" as he analyzes and destroys the experiences of life by reducing them to abstractions. This, again, is the sad result of the devaluation of the feminine intuitive mind. To devaluate one of our two minds is to end up losing the good of the other.[8]

Masculinity, then, is a quality to be experienced—to be glimpsed and tasted as it is passed on from father to son, and yes, even from father to daughter. It is to be celebrated as it descends to us, like darts of joy, through metaphor and symbol, ceremony and ritual. Notice in this verse of William Blake's the capacity of metaphor and symbol to catch the transcendent masculine:

> Bring me my Bow of burning gold:
> Bring me my Arrows of desire:
> Bring me my Spear: O clouds, unfold!
> Bring me my Chariot of fire.

Ultimately masculinity descends to us through the way of love—the way of divine revelation and incarnation. Ultimately masculinity is an attribute of God. Because it is resident in Him, we as Christians can get in touch with it as we abide in Him. God's masculinity can be experienced in prayer, and our own brought to life in us. It is for this reason that healing prayer can be so incredibly effective in even the severest cases, such as Richard's. There is really no case too hard for our God. But we live in a time when poetic and transcendent truth has been long denied, and we have even spent the capital accrued from the combined wisdom of the pagan and the Christian world alike. This is why we moderns know so very little about masculinity (or femininity). In truth, "There's no niche in the world for people that won't be either pagan or Christian,"[9] or for impoverished moderns who fail to grasp the "beyond."

When the "Beyond" Is Denied

Had Richard gone to most present-day counselors, the chances are very great that he would simply have been diagnosed as homosexual and told something akin to this statement I received in the mail today. (Paradoxically it was in a campus ministry newsletter of a large Catholic archdiocese.)

More and more professional people believe that homosexuality is genetic, perhaps a mutation.

The theory behind this statement resembles Freudian theory only insofar as its writer, like Freud, knows "only one nexus between image and 'beyond'—the genetic mechanism."[10] Working "under the influence of the natural sciences," Freud *"had* to reduce symptoms to their biological substratum," as Karl Stern points out.[11] But why would this be the case for a writer representing the church? The statement in this newsletter was not accompanied by a single valid psychological insight (Freud's or anyone else's) on the subject; much less did it contain even the slimmest hint of the *incarnational* view of man and life that the church is based on. What the writer actually attempted, in effect, was to pave the way for retranslating all the Scriptures on the topic of homosexuality by quoting a "professional" who naively stated that we (as well as all ancient and medieval thinkers) have simply misunderstood the Scriptures.

In response to such mindless revisionism as this, Elisabeth Elliot rightly says that we are living in a dangerous time. "It's dangerous and destructive to treat sexuality as if it were meaningless. Much of the church, which is being strongly influenced by the world's ideologies, is ignoring the fact that sexuality means something."[12]

As an individual, Richard's sexuality *meant* something. It had spiritual and psychological as well as physical dimensions. It had, as we have seen, cosmic dimensions that would make all the difference in how he would, if whole, collaborate with the Spirit of God in his own *becoming,* in his own vocation. Had he settled for the current "wisdom," his role in life would have been severely truncated, it would have tunneled hellward down the narcissistic whirlpool of our day. He would never have entered into the Great Dance of loving relationships; he would never have fulfilled his mission in life.

Masculinity and the True or Real Self

Richard was a man who desired the truth. He longed to *do* the truth, to *be* the truth. He longed to participate in the higher meaning of life. He longed to be Christian in thought, word, and deed. But he was cut off from his masculinity, and with it the power of his true self to come forward and to function. Created to function as a *masculine maker* in the image of God, he was a broken image in need of drastic repair. As he failed to realize his masculine identity, the dreadful void in the center of his being widened. It threatened to swallow up the struggling, submerged true self, the *real* Richard, altogether.

Men capable of loving their families, and in possession of their masculine identity, are on the natural plane the chief channels God has ordained for passing manhood on to man. "A man is never a man until his father tells him he is a man," is the way the old folk-saying captures this important psychological insight.

Every boy or girl must separate his or her identity from that of the mother. We are born not knowing that we are separate from our mothers. Slowly we discover this, and begin the hard task of separating our personal and sexual identities from hers. Psychologists point out progressions from infancy to maturity which involve many steps of psychosocial development. There are the usual, normal progressions, and when we miss a step we are in trouble.

The step of self-acceptance ideally comes just after puberty. Puberty/adolescence is the narcissistic stage for all of us. While in it, we are overly concerned and self-conscious about ourselves (especially our bodies) and whether or not we are acceptable to others or to ourselves. This behavior, if we continue to engage in it, translates into the wrong kind of self-love. To achieve a whole, healthy personality, we must pass from this self-centered stage to the self-acceptance that is reasonably full and secure. Whoever does not accept himself (love himself aright) is necessarily turned inward upon himself. To be free to turn outward and love others, I must accept myself.

Whether or not we accept ourselves as persons is dependent upon affirmation coming to us through the masculine voice. I cannot as a woman affirm my son or daughter in his or her gender identity. It is the male voice they are listening for, because as children of my womb they are separating their identity from me. The bonds with the father before this crucial time of adolescence are of course important. Now, however, they are all-important. As the father comes "between" his sons and their mothers where necessary, he enables them to separate their *sexual and personal identities* from hers. This is also true with the daughter, though not quite so crucial insofar as sexual identity is concerned. She is not, after all, *other* than mother.

Dr. Elizabeth Moberly, author of *Psychogenesis* and *Homosexuality: A New Christian Ethic,* states:

> I believe that the relationship with the father is crucial for sexual identity for the boy—but only secondary for the girl, for whom the mother-daughter relationship is of primary significance (I discussed this in detail in *Psychogenesis*). The lesbian has experienced defensive detachment in relation to the mother; once this has happened, the father is unable to reinforce his daugh-

ter's femininity, precisely because there is no longer an ongoing process of female identification (through attachment to the mother) to be reinforced. The task here is to resolve the underlying ambivalence towards the mother and other females, and to meet legitimate developmental needs for (non-sexual) feminine love.[13]

But both sexes listen for the masculine voice at puberty. Whether or not we come out of the narcissistic stage and accept ourselves depends upon the affirmation that comes from the masculine.

When the father's strong hand of love and affirmation does not rest on his son's or daughter's shoulder, tragedy results, especially in this day of the diminished, nuclear family. Effective father substitutes are rare indeed. Grandfathers, uncles, and other masculine role models are even more remote than fathers. Richard had never been affirmed as a man by his father; in fact, in the tangled relationships between his father and his mother, every dimension of his masculinity had lacked affirmation and so was lost to him. It was this loss, and the inner pain of it, that he described as the "flaw" inside himself, one that had deepened into a crack that was steadily giving way under the pressure of life.

Masculinity and the Will of Man

Those who minister in the power that the Holy Spirit gives in healing prayer soon learn to discard ineffective ways of praying. The Holy Spirit's ways are direct and powerful, and sometimes the directions we get are not at all what we would have expected. Those of us who listen closely for such directions know that we are quite fallible, and the leadings we get must be finally judged by the fruit of such prayer, as indeed are prophecy, preaching, or teaching likewise judged. A number of years ago I was strongly led to pray for the release and strengthening of the masculine within a man or woman when the *will* was weak, bound, or passive. The abundance of good fruit produced by such prayer has convinced me that the will is a masculine part of our being.

Without a doubt, masculinity and the true self have a special tie-in to the will of man. Oswald Chambers has written: "The profound thing in man is his will. . . . Will is the essential element in God's creation of man."[14] The *will* is that in man which chooses whether to be or not to be. It is with the will that we choose the heaven of becoming or the hell of failure to become.

In C. S. Lewis's famous book *The Screwtape Letters,* he writes from the point of view of hell. Screwtape, a senior devil, writes directions to Wormwood, a junior tempter intent on devouring a new Christian convert.

> Think of your man as a series of concentric circles, his will being the innermost, his intellect coming next, and finally his fantasy. You can hardly hope, at once, to exclude from all the circles everything that smells of the Enemy: but you must keep on shoving all the virtues outward till they are finally located in the circle of fantasy, and all the desirable qualities inward into the Will. It is only in so far as they reach the will and are there embodied in habits that the virtues are really fatal to us. (I don't, of course, mean what the patient mistakes for his will, the conscious fume and fret of resolutions and clenched teeth, but the real centre, what the Enemy calls the Heart.)[15]

Screwtape, in another letter, finds it necessary to enlarge on this matter of the human will and the centrality of choosing to obey God despite all feelings and circumstances.

He wants them to learn to walk and must therefore take away His hand; and if only the will to walk is really there He is pleased even with their stumbles. Do not be deceived, Wormwood. Our cause is never more in danger than when a human, no longer desiring, but still intending, to do our Enemy's will, looks round upon a universe from which every trace of Him seems to have vanished, and asks why he has been forsaken, and still obeys.[16]

It would be difficult to overemphasize the unique place of man's will, for it stands, as C. S. Lewis says, at the very frontier, that place where man meets God, that place which is "at the mysterious point of junction and separation where absolute being utters derivative being."[17] Here man either wills to relate to his Creator or, turning to love only the self, wills separation.

As a result of the Fall, each man's personality is divided within him and needs to become one before he can know who he is. Lewis rightly saw that whatever else is involved, finally our human will determines whether or not our personality is made one. He expresses this insight in terms of Christ's soul: "This human soul in Him was unswervingly united to the God in Him in that which makes a personality one, namely, *Will*."[18] The human will is linked with the conscious mind of man, which most obviously distinguishes him from the rest of nature. It is consciousness that gives man choice—to obey or not to obey. And it is when man is obedient, when he *wills* to unite himself with God, that he finds himself to be one person—a person whose choices are continually changing him from the very center of his being into that perfected person that shall be.

Such a person's will is magnificently free and may be termed the creative will, for in contrast to a selfish or self-centered will it seeks to interact with all that *is*. Such a person's will is vibrantly alive and active, and may be termed the *masculine will* in that it is infused by the very power and masculinity of God. It is with this masculine, active will that we responsibly and decisively choose. When a man or a woman is cut off from the masculine within, his or her capacity to choose wholeness and heaven is in jeopardy. That man or woman will need prayer for the healing and even (in many cases) deliverance of the will, in its full power to choose, as it is freed and restored to him or her.

As we will to be in Christ, He gathers together the scattered, unaffirmed parts of ourselves from which we are estranged. Just as a man will find his true self only in communion and union with Christ, so too will he find his true masculinity. You may be asking what one does when his will, along with his masculine side, is suppressed and atrophied. This brings us to the unique truth of Christianity: all that is real is incarnational. The eternal Masculine and the Divine Will may *descend* into us and radiate through us, fulfilling and completing our own "natural" faculties. Just as Another's righteousness is ours, so Another's will is ours. St. Augustine, understanding perfectly such an incarnation, prayed in this fashion: "Lord, command what Thou wilt, then *will* what Thou commandest." He understood that what God *wills*, He will do in and through us, and that we are simply to make our weak and insufficient will one with His.

We are already in the higher Will; He is in us. Dante, perhaps the greatest poet of all time, knew this and captured it by saying, "We are *in-willed. In-godded.*" The will, the power to obey, the power to know the truth and do it, speak it, be it, is all in Christ, in our God. This is why when we pray for a person's healing, we always first invoke the Presence of God. In a mighty *sursum corda* we become the catalyst and the channel for the creating, re-creating Light of God. "O send out Thy Light and Thy truth," we pray, "and

enter into this Thy little one and complete him, heal him."
And when a soul, however feeble in will, looks up to Him
with a heart open to receive, it receives from His own store
that which is needed. He descends into the frail human will,
joining it with His, and the strengthening, healing work is
done.

This morning, meditating on the awesomeness of true
masculinity and the fact that it is an attribute of God, I
wrote out the following prayer in my journal:

> Lord, send me Your wisdom regarding masculinity and
> its tie-in with the will, with authority. Father, Holy
> Father, Thou art all truth and righteousness. All au-
> thority, wisdom, truth, and justice are Yours. Truly, You
> are so masculine, we are all feminine in relation to You.
> I know this can never be fully understood, but please,
> Father, more nearly define for me what Your masculin-
> ity is.

And these were the words as they came quickly and
with great clarity to my heart:

> Masculinity is the *power* to do good. I am all good-
> ness. But I am also powerful, all-powerful. My power
> to do that which is good, which is holy, which is
> righteous, is My "masculine." The perverted masculine
> on the earthly plane is the power to *do* turned to a
> selfish or self-serving cause. When Jesus said: "All
> power is given unto Me in heaven and earth" we see
> the masculine at its ultimate. Every knee will bow be-
> fore this ultimate power and authority.

Like Mary, we hide such words as these in our hearts
and await their confirmation. Although we believe them, we
make no specious claims concerning them. We realize that

we can know only in part and through a glass darkly, as St. Paul says. One thing is certain, however. To be in touch with one's masculinity at the highest level is to be empowered with Truth Himself. It is to be enabled to take one's stand (no matter what the circumstances) against the lies and the illusions of one's individual life and environment as well as the lies and illusions of one's corporate existence and age.

Masculinity and Truth

When enough individuals are out of touch with the masculine, a whole society is weakened on every level of existence. Alexander Solzhenitsyn gives us a good idea of how Western society, in which this problem is pandemic, can be perceived by someone with a fresh perspective. He says of the West that we are

> too weak to oppose the Communist evil that overcomes and defies intelligent thinking:—that we have let ourselves be pushed into the trench dug out for us by communism because of our spiritual weakness. . . . Western society as it appears today, which is consuming more and more, shying away from work, hedonistic, whose family is destroying itself, tempted by drugs, atheistic, paralyzed by terrorism, has spent its vital energy and lost its spiritual health. It cannot survive such as it is.

"One word of truth outweighs the world," said Solzhenitsyn in his famous Nobel speech. And we, in the clutches of this crisis, cannot effectively hear or speak the truth. In response to writers hinting that communism, as an ideology, is dying, Solzhenitsyn said:

> Before dying it will yet find enough time to destroy and conquer the whole West and relish in its blood. Com-

munist ideology is a metaphysical force that runs counter to nature. It acts in defiance of physical, economic and sociological laws. Instead of perishing, as it should, it goes triumphant. It is triumphant because of the West's weakness.

Solzhenitsyn would not have spent the energy to write and speak these words had he not yet hope that men would stand and be empowered by God, that men would yet do battle and win against the metaphysical force (a demonic atheism by whatever name it takes) that desires above all to cut man off from the transcendent by denying the "beyond."

A crisis in masculinity is always a crisis in truth. It is a crisis in *powerlessness* of the feminine virtues: the good, the beautiful, and the just, in a culture or in an individual. A culture will never become decadent in the face of a healthy, balanced masculinity. When a nation or an entire Western culture backslides, it is the masculine which is first to decline.

5 The Polarity and Complementarity of the Sexes

There ought spiritually to be a man in every woman and a woman in every man. And how horrid ones who haven't got it are: I can't bear a "man's man" and a "woman's woman." (C. S. Lewis, letter to Sr. Penelope)

"Masculine and feminine can be understood only in terms of each other; basically they are opposite and complementary qualities." So said my friend, the poet-novelist Robert Siegel. With the clarity and the insight of the poet, he continued on, "They are like darkness and light. It is very hard to understand darkness except in terms of light, and light except in terms of darkness. They are two extremes on a continuum."

Our Bipolar Nature
God said, "We will make man in Our image, after Our likeness" (Genesis 1:26, literal Hebrew).

Unity arises out of polarity. The highest expression of this is the idea that man is androgynous (male-female) in his origin and his final destination. The most famous presentation of this idea is found in Genesis when God created man in His image, "male and female"—*before* the separation of Eve out of the body of Adam. This, according to Christian tradition, indicates the androgynous nature of the Godhead Himself—meaning, again, that here *polarity in union* is the expression of fullness of being.[1]

We should also remember that there is a false androgyny, proclaimed especially by certain feminist and homosexual activists. These people proclaim that there are no significant differences between male and female, that biological facts and imagery simply do not matter. Even some Christian feminists come near to saying this. But their view is misguided and not in correspondence with reality.

Masculinity and femininity are attributes of God, and we, in His image, are most surely—in our spiritual, psychological, and physical beings—bipolar creatures. Our Creator, holding all that is true and real within Himself, reflects both the masculine and the feminine, and so do we. The more nearly we function in His image, the more nearly we reflect both the masculine and the feminine in their proper balance—that is, in the differing degrees and aptitudes appropriate to our sexual identities as male and female.

The Hebrew word for woman is *ish shah,* and is apparently a word play by the sacred writer on the term for man, *ish.* Although the two words have different etymologies, even so this word play points to the fact that woman too is man—*she man, womb-man,* or *female man.* To be whole, not only must her femininity be affirmed, but the masculine side within her needs to be recognized, balanced, and strengthened where necessary. Man and woman are both healed in the same way—by seeing with the eyes of the heart (or the true imagination) the Unseen Real, by listening to God and doing what they hear Him say.

The woman who sits and worships at the feet of Jesus, like Mary of Bethany, and who learns to obey (initiate) what she hears Him say, will not only find her femininity affirmed in all its splendid dimensions, but will also begin to get in touch with the masculine side of herself. Elisabeth Elliot, in line with the best wisdom of the ages, states that "the essence of masculinity is initiation and the essence of femininity is response." For a woman to be free to initiate—free, that is, to hear the word of the Lord and do what she hears Him say—is for her to be in touch with her masculine side. She is not sickly passive—the feminine principle estranged from the masculine. She is free to respond to God with all her being, and therefore able to *initiate* when the occasion calls for it. In the upright, vertical relationship to her Lord, she is fully a person, fully enabled to collaborate with His Spirit. She is a balanced feminine *maker* in the image of her Creator Father.

Likewise, for a man to fully function as a masculine *maker*, he must be in touch with the feminine principle in him. His heart must be capable of *responding* to God, to others, to the work that is to be done. His heart, like that of his female counterpart's, is the fertile womb that continually receives the life of Christ and in response gives birth to the *making* God has ordained him to do. Listening obediently for the healing word that God is always sending, he becomes a servant and steward of that word, a nurturer of it in the hearts of others. He therefore becomes a healer of broken relationships. He is the masculine *bride* of God.

Invariably when a soul needs healing there will be an imbalance within of the masculine and the feminine. He or she is tipping the scales too far toward one extreme of the continuum. This imbalance of the power to initiate and the power to respond can always be healed when a person forsakes his *vision and will in separation from God* (what the Scripture calls dying to the old man), comes into the Presence, and there unites with the incredible realities outside himself.

Learning about Gender Differences

I grew up in a household of women, my father having died when I had barely turned three. Besides myself and my mother, he left my sister, an infant of eighteen months. My widowed maternal grandmother then joined us. So we were three generations of feminine souls under one roof. When uncles or male cousins visited, my litle sister and I viewed them with respect and awe, and in some cases with fear and trepidation. Men could be very unpredictable where the affairs of little children were concerned. Grandmother proudly catered to them while we stood back and watched. Once in a while I'd be asked to go to the piano and play a piece for them, or sent to fetch some drawing or bit of schoolwork for their scrutiny and approval. I longed to please them (as I did anyone else), and was occasionally allowed to serve them a cup of coffee or a piping hot cinnamon roll. But for many years men remained to me as foreign and inscrutable as creatures from another planet. In my childhood they were simply outside my intimate experience and knowledge.

It came to me as a shock therefore to later discover what I've come to call the "drive toward power" inherent in the healthy young male. The grandiose ideas are there in the mind, and all the energy of the young masculine body is ready to serve the ideas if only the proper channel to do so can be found. Truly we are made to serve a cause greater than ourselves. The drive toward power in the male, out of touch with a cause greater than that of fulfilling and thus quieting his own ego needs, can be a fearful thing indeed.

This, as I came to realize later, is the plight of a man

out of touch with the feminine principle within and without and *therefore*, paradoxically, out of touch with the transcendent Masculine. For example, a young man in the throes of such a drive must come present to his own heart—his feminine intuitive side, that part of him that can see, hear, and respond to God. Otherwise he is in danger of becoming the little Napoleon in his orbit, whether his orbit is in the ministry, law, the military, or whatever. As has been said: "War represents an excess of masculine initiative unrefined by feminine wisdom."[2]

I first received insight into this masculine predicament when I began teaching college students "listening prayer," that important but much neglected step of prayer I talk about in *The Broken Image*.[3] To my amazement and grief, in their "listening" these young men, rather than coming present to their own hearts in such a way as to *know* them and receive the word God was speaking, would hear this "drive toward power" verbalizing itself. They would come up with grandiose notions of great exploits (notions that, of course, have to be distinguished from the truly great works that Christians are commissioned to do). And since these were gifted, idealistic young Christian men, their fantasies would be on the order of "conquering the world for Jesus" single-handedly.

The young women had their problems in listening prayer as well, and these centered around matters concerning the affairs of the heart—their most cherished romantic notions of what it meant to be chosen and loved by a husband. They would come to me saying, "Guess what! The Lord just told me who I am going to marry!"

And I would ask, "Did He tell the young man?"

"Well, no."

Here we see the feminine predicament: the normal feminine drive to receive and respond to the male is in remarkable contrast to the masculine drive toward power. In such a case it is usually safe to say that the strong gender drive within the young woman is speaking so loudly that she fails to differentiate its voice from the quieter wisdom which comes from God. All this, being a woman, I could readily understand and help with. But what was this in the male? Growing up in a household of women had in no way prepared me to understand these men, though it had given me a unique basis from which to contrast certain critical differences between men and women.

As I prayed with these earnest young men, I began to realize that what I saw as an unexplainable and troubling "drive toward power" in the matter of spiritual exploits was really only part of a basic masculine principle (in this case immature and unrestrained) that characterizes the male attitudinally, intellectually, and biologically. To quote Karl Stern again:

> Just as in the function of the spermatozoon in its relation to the ovum, man's attitude toward nature is that of attack and penetration. He removes rocks and uproots forests to make space for agriculture. He dams rivers and harnesses the power of water.[4]

Intellectually the polarity of the sexes corresponds to a polarity in the human ways of *knowing*—that of the masculine discursive reason and of the feminine intuitive mind. In the disciplines requiring analytical as over against intuitive intelligence, men excel and lead the way. Here again we see the "drive toward power," the masculine principle at work.

> Chemistry breaks up the compound of molecules and rearranges the position of atoms. Physics *overcomes* the law of nature, gravity, first in the invention of the wheel—last in the suprasonic rocket which soars into the stratosphere. Even in the realm of thought, in philosophy and in pure mathematics, the "nature" of things is being pierced."[5]

The feminine principle, on the other hand, is more deeply rooted in the unconscious ways of knowing, the heart's way, and a woman's physiology reflects the principle.

> Just as in sexual physiology the female principle is one of receiving, keeping and nourishing—woman's *specific* form of creativeness, that of motherhood, is tied up with the life of nature, with a *non-reflective bios.*[6]

Helen Deutsch and others speak

> of a form of *knowledge* or *awareness* which is not only independent of reason but goes beyond it. The sociologist Georg Simmel remarks that for woman "being and idea are indivisibly one." . . . [F]or him [man] the idea can be conceived only as an outside and an above: it is not immanent. It is in a very similar sense that Jean Guitton observes that love, as a natural gift, is a characteristic element of all womanhood. . . . [I]ntuitive intelligence is more intimately tied up with love than analytical intelligence. Hence, woman's "strength is the intuitive grasp of the living concrete; especially of the personal element. She has the special gift of making herself at home in the inner world of others."[7]

It was not some culturally induced behavior that I had happened on in attempting to teach young men and women to listen to God and to their own hearts, for it went to the roots of spirit, soul, and body. In their behavior was to be seen the "fundamental duality which remains immutable at the bottom of all cultural variants,"[8] and this duality was striving toward satisfaction and resolution. It was what both moderns and ancients wise in the way of the masculine and the feminine have always known in every culture.

The sex organs and the sex cells manifest a polarity and complementarity in morphology and in function. In the act of sexual union the male organ is convex and penetrating and the female organ is concave and receptive; the spermatozoon is torpedo-shaped and "attacks," and the ovum is a sphere "awaiting" penetration. That this polarity and complementariness should not be confined to the physical but also be reflected in the character of man and woman, is a view as old as history. As a matter of fact, in ancient religions and philosophies, sexual polarity and complementariness did not stop at the psychological. Human duality and human mating expressed an antithesis at the very heart of things, an antithesis striving for synthesis unceasingly, eternally—in an act of anticipation and restitution of unity. This tradition is so ubiquitous and abundant that one could not possibly present it here in detail. The most remarkable thing about it is perhaps the fact that it is expressed in religions and philosophies widely separated in time and place. We find the idea clearly expressed in Taoism and in the Sohar, in the Upanishads and in Christianity. Events in nature and in human history are explained by two principles. In Taoism these are *Yin*—the feminine which is calm, dark and receptive, and *Yang*—the male which is active, light and generative. An eternal movement of reciprocity between the two is safeguarded by a higher principle of oneness, the *Tao.* The rich erotic mysticism of the Kabbala shows a striking resemblance to the Chinese tradition. Heaven as *Tiph'ereth* is the male principle which, through the arms of the world, is in union with earth as *Malchuth,* the womanly principle. Unity arises out of polarity. The highest expression of this is the idea that man is androgynous (male-female) in his origin and his final destination. The most famous presentation of this idea is found in Genesis when God created man in His image, "male and female"—*before* the separation of Eve out of the body of Adam. This, according to Christian tradition, indicates the androgynous nature of the Godhead Himself—meaning, again, that here *polarity in union* is the expression of fullness of being. No less famous is the development of the same idea in the speech of Aristophanes in Plato's *Symposium:* man and woman, in the sexual embrace, restitute the primary unity of the human person in its fullness, a unity which has, at one time, been broken. It is remarkable that here for once, before the Christian epoch, Greek and Jew agree. The same idea had already been presented in the Upanishads: "But He, too, Athman (soul, God) had no joy, for He was as big as Man and Woman are together when they unite. Then his substance was divided into two parts, from whence came Man and Woman. Hence the body, too, is a 'half.' " There exists a similar Assyrian version. Indeed, it would not be surprising to find that this is, among esoteric traditions, the only universal one. Of course, if it were so it could easily be explained: the very existence of men and women is the one constant in all civilizations. Our metaphysical sense tells us with the irreducible immediacy of sensory perception, that this invariability *means* something, apart from all shifting contingencies.[9]

Having started to pray with the college students, I was forced to grow leaps and bounds as a spiritual director in order to help the young men and women I prayed with come present to their own hearts and there learn to read them aright. Each would have to know and understand himself *as man* and *as woman* in order to keep the strong drives associated with gender identity from getting in the way of obedience to God. While acknowledging and by no means denying the drive, they would have to, in the fashion of St. Paul, "bring the body under" (1 Corinthians 9:27). In other words, they would have to "die to" these drives at one level so a resurrection could take place—that is, so the mature (unselfish or unself-centered) masculine and feminine might come forth within them, achieving a wholesome integration.

The young men, in coming present to their own hearts, would recognize the overweening ego needs (or the lack of an ego-image) behind their grandiose ambitions of conquering the world and thereby proving themselves as men. Much later I began to realize their need as part of a general crisis in masculinity—that of the unaffirmed male. Their condition had not been unhealthy in the sense of being abnormal. It was simply the way of the masculine when it is yet immature and striving for affirmation. Theirs was the condition of the egocentric masculine will untempered by the transcendent Masculine Will. It was man attempting to find affirmation, self-acceptance, and identity in what he could accomplish, by himself rather than in union with God.

Up to a point, of course, their striving was normal and related to the masculine principle itself. We all, men and women alike, need a tough struggle in order to prove our mettle, and life itself soon provides it. Unless some unwise soul attempts to do our struggling for us and forever cushions the blows that life provides, we soon discover that it is precisely the hard places in life that make or break us. It is in learning to persevere through the really tough times that we grow in resolve (the masculine *will* to choose life and wholeness), in moral and spiritual discipline (the feminine *wisdom* to choose aright), and in the understanding of our own hearts and the hearts of others. The problem here, of course, is that success in overcoming the hard places in life does not finally satisfy. There comes a time when we realize that true identity is not to be found in what we can do, but in our ability to obey and respond to Someone far greater than ourselves. But the struggle to overcome is normal and not to be bypassed.

An illustration of the above was provided by a very capable and successful young man who had just found Christ in meetings I was holding in his city. He later proved to be one of the leaders in Christian renewal in his parish and in his section of the country. "I am so glad," he said, "that you didn't come here before now, not even last year. I would never have been able to hear you. I had to prove myself first."

I understood perfectly what he meant. Before this time all his attention was given to proving himself a man. He had gone through the hard places and had prevailed. And he had had sufficient time to know that succeeding financially and professionally, as well as in his role as husband and father, was not enough. In fact, he was headed in the direction of being bored with it all, an *ennui* he instinctively knew to be the fertile ground for a little more social drinking every year and perhaps even marital unrest on down the road. Then he had come present to his own heart and had begun to know it. He could therefore hear me when I proclaimed Christ as the way, the truth, and the life, the only One in whom he could find his ultimate masculinity and true identity.

This was precisely the place the young men I was teaching needed to come to. In the meantime, they were still outwardly (though unconsciously) concerned with proving themselves as men, and they were in danger of attempting to find their identity, not in Christ, but in spiritual exploits. They would have to come present to their own hearts. Their spiritual condition was that of the masculine not in touch with the feminine, intuitive side which hears and responds to the will and word of God. *Theirs was the very condition listening prayer sets out to remedy.*

The unhealthy male is the one in whom this drive toward power is so repressed that it cannot come forth, much less die and find itself resurrected in the presence of God. This is the masculine plight that we as ministers and counselors find ourselves facing in ever-increasing numbers of men from every walk of life. This is the condition, in widely varying degrees, that this book seeks to address. Its thesis is that men are no longer simply involved in what Karl Stern has so correctly and brilliantly chronicled as "the flight from woman." In his book he plots the historical and philosophical course that led the male of this century into a restless and uncommitted activism: a lack of balance between action and contemplation due to his rejection of the feminine—within himself and within his female counterpart. Karl Stern, as a learned student of history, philosophy, and science, correctly diagnosed the problem, and as a physician-psychiatrist he faced the psychological suffering it brought about in his patients and in the culture at large.

But the masculine plight that Karl Stern wrote about, having gone uncorrected, has now greatly worsened. Having for so many generations undervalued the feminine, men are in general now increasingly cut off from their masculine side and are trapped in the sickly passive—that which is the feminine state when it is unhealthy and cut off from the masculine. We cannot lose the feminine principle without weakening and eventually losing the masculine; we cannot retain the good of the masculine discursive reason apart from the feminine intuitive mind and heart. All the precious and colorful strands of reality are wonderfully interconnected. To discard one strand is to loosen and thereby endanger the whole framework of life.

Although many men who seek help will still be found in the throes of the activism Karl Stern writes about, they will now more often be seen floundering, to one extent or another, in an overly developed feminine side, which is a caricature of the feminine. Rather than striving to find their identity and worth in what they achieve (whether it is wealth, social standing, professional status, sexual conquests, or whatever), many fall into a more or less paralyzed state. Instead of being in touch with and knowing their own hearts—their genuinely gifted, feminine, intuitive side—they simply exist, caught in the throes of a passive and uncreative suffering.

The masculine and the feminine within man and within woman, by whatever name they are called, or by whatever they are understood to be, seek recognition, affirmation, and proper balance. Much that is called emotional illness or instability today, as I continually discover in prayer and counseling sessions, is merely the masculine and/or the feminine unaffirmed and out of balance within the personality. *Merely* is always, as C. S. Lewis has said, a dangerous word, and it surely is in this case if one does not recognize the potentially fatal blow an imbalance of the masculine and the feminine can wield, whether to the health of an individual, a society, or an entire civilization. In fact, there is profound ontological significance in this matter of the essential polarity of the sexes and of the masculine and the feminine genders. To disregard their complementariness, out of which issues fullness of being on the natural plane, is finally to strike a blow at the true self in every man—indeed, at *being* itself. This is what I have increasingly come to realize as I pray with people in need of psychological healing. It is precisely as Karl Stern has said:

> Human anguish is never entirely explained biologically or psychologically. There remains an ontological sediment: the tension of Man stretched eternally between being and non-being.[10]

Gender participates in the mystery of *being* itself. And in the anguish of the human person—stretched to whatever degree between being and nonbeing—his or her masculine or feminine identity and the balance with its polar opposite are always to be reckoned with.

6 Woman in Crisis: The Story of Richard's Wife and Others

In the psychic budget of the individual the two compo-
nents, male and female, must be "linked in harmony."
What "linked in harmony" actually means cannot be
easily explained without going into a great amount of
clinical observation. At any rate, *lack of integration,
unbalance of the two principles leads to a "troubled
destiny."* Coleridge made the statement, amazing for his
time: "The truth is, a great mind must be androgynous." This holds for everybody, not only "a great
mind," but in a way we cannot yet define with clinical
precision [italics mine]. (Karl Stern)[1]

Richard's lovely and wonderfully feminine wife, Renie,
wanting to find wholeness, needed prayer for the healing of
her will, in order to be in touch with and have permission to
use the good of her reasoning, analytical, masculine mind.
This healing would not make her any the less feminine.
Rather, it would assure the good of her feminine side and
enable her to avoid the pitfalls that both her mother and
Richard's had fallen into.

Richard's mother, bound to her own passivity, and unable to initiate creative change, is a graphic example of woman unhealed in a number of ways, but especially in her *will*. Dwelling in a paralyzed state of no more "becoming," she represents for us what the ancient doctors of the soul called "accedia" or spiritual sloth—a state that ends in the refusal of all joy. She is woman cut off from her masculine side, the side that could enable her to come out of the bog of her subjective feelings, the hell of self and self-pity, the miasma of the ersatz feminine. Richard's mother-in-law provides another frightening picture of alienation from the healthy masculine within woman.

Renie was the only child of an utterly possessive mother. This mother is an example of the woman who, separated from her masculine side, is subject to the ersatz masculine. She is the female who is not free to become, and whose creative energies erupt therefore at a lower level—that of a dominating, manipulative love toward her husband and children. Separated from the good of reason, from healthy initiative, and from the power to rejoice in a world outside her own subjective cosmos, she concentrates on those within her closed orbit. Although she can never find her identity and fulfillment in her husband or her children, she endlessly demands it of them.

Richard's wife had never been able to get free of her mother's demands, and constantly battled feelings of guilt over being unable to do enough to please her mother. Although she did not realize it, she needed her identity separated from that of her mother. She needed prayer that would 1) free her to forsake the position of living out of the guilty little girl who was always trying to survive her mom's devouring love; and 2) equally as important, she needed prayer that would enable her to live from the Center, to live securely and joyously from that place *within* where her true self dwelt in union with her God. This, of course, would bring about a proper balance of the masculine and the feminine within her essentially responsive female self.

A letter from Renie, received after her healing, tells her story. Her own healing came several months after her husband's, at a time when she was in a state of awe and utter thanksgiving to God over what had happened to him, and over the continuing presence of God and His healing in their marriage. Hers was a profoundly religious awe—an awe which comes only with the power to believe and receive from God.

But before her visit to my home, and in their new state of joyful *becoming* as a couple, they had gone for a holiday visit back to her parents' home. During this visit, their new-found joy and freedom proved an additional threat to her parents, and Renie realized more deeply than ever before the seriousness and the scope of her problems with her mother. Subsequently she came for healing prayer, and afterward, as she was leaving, I suggested she write out her story and send it to me. I often do this, for it not only helps me to see how well the person has understood and received the prayers said over him, but it further strengthens that person's understanding of himself or herself and God's grace at work in his life.

It is a wonderful thing to be able to tell the true tale of our lives. And writing it out not only forces us to think it through more clearly, but opens our hearts to new "seeings," new understandings. In C. S. Lewis's book *Till We Have Faces,* his protagonist, Orual, is "drenched with seeings." After inner healing prayer, people are often drenched with seeings. Once the revelations begin, they continue as the conditions of prayer and quiet are continued.

Prayerfully writing out our own story is often the key that opens greater doors to our understanding of it, and this was so for Renie. For this reason alone, I am happy that Renie followed through on my suggestion, but also because her letter reveals the need women have to get *their* identities separated from that of their mother. It also reveals some of the hazards in a woman's life who is out of sufficient touch with her masculine side and at the mercy of her responsive but overly passive essential feminine self.

Renie's Letter

"My healing began when I got back from our trip to my parents' home for a month. Your book *The Broken Image* was in our overflowing mail. Richard read through it first, and after a few days I was able to start reading. I was fascinated from the start, but it really began to penetrate to my spirit when I got to the section on 'Lesbian Relationships,' particularly the pages dealing with possessive and dominating mothers. The more I read, the more astonished I became, as for the first time in my thirty-one years someone was describing my relationship to my mother. Although my relationship with my mom had not led to a lesbian problem, I knew it was unhealthy, and it totally frustrated me.

"I shared this realization with Richard, and we both agreed I should pursue a meeting with you in order to try to get to the bottom of my continuing burden concerning my mom.

"Richard made the arrangements to come see you, and I began to get excited in a deep, heartfelt way. I began to feel for the first time in my life that there *was* light at the end of this tunnel.

"We arrived at your door, and you greeted us in a loving, relaxed, and open way. That greeting helped to calm my nerves. I was feeling what the children in C. S. Lewis's Narnia stories must have felt whenever they encountered Aslan. They knew he was not a tame lion, and that they had to come clean with him! I knew I must unveil myself to you in order to get to the core of this problem. But my anxiousness to find a solution to a lifelong bafflement gave me courage to tell it all.

"Having read your book, I knew I needed to go as far back in the past as I could possibly remember in order to tell my story.

"I was the only child of a couple who had finally conceived after ten years of marriage. Many times I was told how difficult it was for Mom to become pregnant. She knew exactly the night of my conception because she and Dad had tried a new method of placing a pillow under Mom's pelvis so that her position would be perfectly placed to conceive. She then remained in that position all night so as not to lose any sperm. This story was always hard for me to hear, for it was told with certain 'implications,' or so it seemed to me. It made me feel I had caused them so much effort that I'd better live up to their expectations.

"All my life I had tried to shoulder the tensions between a negative personality (my mom), and a happy-go-lucky personality (my dad). I never knew our home to be free from tension unless we had company or were all directing our attention to the TV. Consequently, we watched television nonstop every night. Mother would complain that we never talked to her, but whenever I did, I felt like I was being coerced. So instead of feeling free to share, I felt forced to give away parts of myself that I would have liked to hold on to. A feeling of being sucked into a vacuum (my mom) was always my reaction.

"My folks did all they could to provide me with a comfortable and varied childhood. My father was always a figure of affirmation to me, and someone I could share with if and when we were ever alone. He was an insurance adjuster, which meant he had to drive many miles a day throughout the state to see people. He seemed happy to be able to serve others this way, and some of my fondest memories are of being allowed to go with him once or twice each summer. The joy of being alone with Dad, away from Mother's dominating eye, was a true release.

"Although Mom was much more possessive with my

time than other mothers, I wrote it off to my being an only child. For example, on the Friday nights when my friends and I had sleepovers at one of their houses, I would awaken early on a Saturday morning to hear Mother honking the horn for me to leave. Sometimes it meant missing breakfast to get out to the car, although the others all stayed till 10:00 A.M. Mom said she came to get me early because I needed to start cleaning the house, which was how I spent every Saturday morning I can remember while growing up. In some ways I enjoyed cleaning, as it gave me a chance at some privacy. As I ran the ancient old Hoover in the seclusion of the living room, I had a chance to think alone. Sometimes I'd get through fast and just let the cleaner run in order to stretch the time of privacy longer. My only private moments were when I was cleaning house, or in the bathroom (at times this was interrupted too!). I would read for hours on end in order to be alone.

"By the time I reached adolescence, I began to see my folks a little more objectively. But I still felt a continual sense of guilt in not being able to fill the lonely vacuum within my mom, no matter how hard I tried. I began to rebel in secret ways, never obvious ones because that would be too difficult to handle. I also began to see that Mom and Dad had no sex life and that this didn't seem to bother them. One day Mom pointed at two dogs mating and announced to me, 'That's how humans do it when they want to have babies.' I felt totally repulsed and yet did not reject my own sexuality. I knew from this and other remarks that she didn't enjoy sex with my dad.

"Whenever Mom and I had a disagreement in my teen-age years, it ended with her accusing me of being too sensitive, and with her crying on Daddy's shoulder. She would say that we were never going to be best friends like she wanted.

"My mom wanted me to go to the junior college in a

neighboring town rather than to the state university four or five hours away. I desperately wanted to go to the university because Dad had attended there and in order to have some measure of independence from the folks.

"My folks were finally persuaded to let me go, and I began the summer immediately following graduation from high school. That summer and the first year I really made up for lost time in socializing with my peers. I joined a sorority, was elected sweetheart to a fraternity, and settled into the typical coed life. In spite of all this, I felt totally split, because every three weeks I was expected to go home for the weekend—no matter what my circumstances were. Also I was expected to write a letter once a week, and to make do on $5.00 per week spending money. If by chance I couldn't find a ride home when the third weekend rolled around, and of course I had no money to ride the train, Mom would get on the phone and call around until she located 'somebody' (whether it be a professor or a complete stranger), and arrange a ride for me.

"I became a Christian at the end of my freshman year through a church retreat. Although I had been raised in the Presbyterian church, I had never understood that salvation wasn't based on my merit or performance, but only on faith in Christ's atoning work (death and resurrection.) I began to get involved in Inter-Varsity (a Christian organization), and my folks were excited over my change in lifestyle as long as it didn't take me away from them.

"I met Richard through Inter-Varsity and began dating him my sophomore year, and on into the summer. We were immediately 'kindred spirits,' and soon realized we needed to slow down the relationship for some measure of control. Because of this, we stopped dating in our junior year.

"About this time Dad asked me to write home more often as he felt Mom was on the verge of a mental breakdown over my not being at home anymore. I had visions of Mom ending up in the mental hospital in the town where I was attending college. I then tried a test to see if they would ever be satisfied with me: I decided to write them a letter every day for a whole semester. This did nothing to help, and it only once brought a word of thanks for writing more often.

"Also about this time Mom and Dad decided to move to the city where I was in college. They said this move was in order to redecorate an old house just off campus and rent it out to students, but I knew it was just a further effort to hang on to me. On the day they drove up to sign the papers (bringing a carload of household goods with them), I was late meeting them at the house due to an important date. This sent Mom into a fury, saying that obviously I didn't want them to move up or I would have been sure to get there on time. They left in a huff with Mom in tears and with me feeling tremendous guilt because I really didn't want them to move up in the first place. I never thought it was a smart move, and I knew it was only what it turned out to be, a temporary crutch for them.

"When I graduated from college, I announced to the folks I was spending the summer out east working with an Inter-Varsity group. Because I had saved my money to finance the trip, they agreed to my going. I became involved with this group initially due to Richard's encouragement to do so, but also with the knowledge that I'd have to sign on for a year to be committed to following the advice of my 'leader' rather than my folks. I saw this as a possible way out of my folks' possessiveness, a somewhat gradual way.

"I began to teach school in the town where I lived with two other girls involved in this Christian organization. Soon the old tensions with Mom and Dad raised their heads. They wanted me home at times when I'd have to refuse due to prior commitments to the organization. The folks went round and round with the guy in charge of our group, but soon realized they couldn't order him around as they did me. Several scenes occurred that year, followed by my guilt feelings for bringing pain to my folks, but also resentment against them.

"Richard and I became engaged that year, which gave me tremendous happiness and lightened my problems with the folks, even though it added another strain with them. (The folks, as I well knew, preferred that I marry a secure home-town type.)

"I had been in love with Richard for five years, most of that time spent apart; so I was thrilled that God had brought us together. That helped me get past what the folks thought.

"After eight years of marriage, however, and still head over heels in love with Richard, I still felt tied to my folks and in bondage to their whims and desires. This brings me up to when I came to see you, Leanne.

"I told you most of this story, feeling your complete attention given to it, while your confirmation that I was right in feeling trapped and unable to move in my relationship to my folks relieved me. We then prayed knowing that I was going to be set free of the burden I had carried for thirty-one years.

"One of the first memories that came to the fore, and this surprised me, was of an incident my folks had told me about. As a six-month-old I nearly died and was hospitalized for several weeks. This turned out to be a memory that needed healing. You invited Jesus into that memory, and he healed me of the fear and pain.

"We moved on in prayer to the memory where my mom showed me the dogs having sex, and we prayed for my problem of always seeing sex as dirty. You had me listen for Jesus' word to me of what sex was, and the word I got from

Him is still written in my memory, as well as in my prayer journal. It was just the understanding I needed to change my way of looking at sex.

"Then we moved on to my main problem: Mom's possessiveness. You asked me to picture her, and when I did an ugly, gnarled face that was also my mom's came into my mind and you had me ask God to forgive her. You later said this 'unbidden image' I received was my heart's way of picturing the 'diseased form of mother-love' that I was reacting to. After I forgave my mother, you prayed that I might get my identity separated from hers. [Although Renie doesn't tell about this prayer in detail, it was one in which we asked the Lord to enable us to discern, and then to break, any and all oppressing bondages that had kept her in emotional and spiritual bondage to her mother. We prayed for the healing of her will, and for its full separation from that of her mother's. For more detail on this prayer, see Judith's story later in this chapter. In the following paragraphs, she writes of the main area of bondage and of its being broken.]

"As you prayed for me, you 'saw' a net of manipulation which had been over me even before my conception and birth. By the power of the Spirit in prayer, you cut the net from around me so that I would be free to see my folks objectively rather than subjectively. And I was truly freed from that 'net'; I could see myself crawl right out from under it! At one point you told me I need never go home again unless I wanted to, and those words brought a flood of tears, tears of joy. We laughed together over the relief those words brought to me. I was beginning to know I was independent from my folks for the first time in my life. Later you explained that I need never go home out of a sense of guilt, but only from a 'position of strength,' and that as I looked to the Lord, the time would come when I would not react subjectively to their demands on me, and would be able even to minister to them.

"You then prayed for me to be baptized in the Spirit, anointing my head with oil. I felt like I was floating. As you prayed that my ears might hear the Lord's voice, I had to cry out and thank God for the ability to hear that I now knew I would experience. You prayed for my will to be strengthened to do always that which is right, that which the Lord guides me to do, and which is best for everyone, my folks included.

"As we prayed, I had a vision of myself and the Holy Spirit dancing off into the distance together in a series of twirls. You were seeing this same vision, and we were amazed at the mystery of it all.

"I left your apartment in a daze of joy and deep peace. Richard was astonished over the change in my entire being and rejoiced over every word as I retold our prayer to him. Since praying for this healing, I finally feel my age. Always in the past, I felt immature whenever with others my age. I feel in charge of my life for the first time, and this has taken a huge load off Richard and consequently off our marriage.

"Each day I'm learning new insights about who I am before God. I am able to have two-way conversations with Him that I never knew possible before my healing. His presence is such an ever-present source of strength that I can't imagine life lived without this reservoir.

"I truly feel like a new Renie, able to actively choose rather than passively repress.

"My folks have resisted my independence from them, but as I choose to obey God and do only what He tells me to do, I find that His love brings freedom.

"This has also rearranged my relationship with my folks so that we have begun to relate as peers rather than in an authority/subject position. The healing has brought to the fore the masculine side of myself that had been submerged all these years, and I find it a challenge to encourage that side of myself to grow stronger. Sometimes the old Renie wants to cling to the pseudo-security that the familiar passive side held for me, but this false way of living life is in fact death."

Freeing Woman to Become

There is no longer an incapacitating gender imbalance in Renie's life. She is free to objectively look at each situation in her life as it arises, confer with her husband and others whose wisdom she prizes, consider it prayerfully and intelligently, and *initiate* the changes that are needed. She no longer, out of a sense of dependence and immaturity, does simply what her parents or someone else is pressuring her to do, even though it is in her basic nature as a woman to respond to the needs of others. In touch with the masculine, she is now (two years later) increasingly free to fully *become* the woman she was created to be. Although her father was unable to free her (or himself) from the domination of her mother and thus finally affirm her as a mature person, she found her freedom in Christ.

The difference between Renie and the older women in her family was that she managed to get help. Had she not gotten the help, she would have ended up not knowing the difference between the kind of mother-love that frees and that which devours. She would have continued to be separate from the good of her masculine side, and eventually have been given over to the ersatz masculine. Even though she hated what her mother had done to her, she was already seeing her mom "come through" in herself as she dealt with her own children. Unfree herself, she would hardly know how to free her children.

There is a very great need for the ministry of inner healing in the church, for the gifted but "bound" Renies crowd our church benches. One can only wonder at the persons either Richard's or Renie's mother would have become had they received the prayer help they needed. Both grew up in the church and attended faithfully all their lives. It is wonderful to see women who have suffered such blocks to *becoming* as these suffered blossom after their healing into leaders in the Christian community. To set them free to become 1) the persons they were intended to be, and 2) the "mothers in Israel" who instruct and set others free should be a prime task and goal of the leadership of the church. There must, in other words, be effective feminine disciples as well as masculine ones; only then will men as well as women come into the fullness of their vocation in Christ. (Men, apart from whole women, cannot fulfill their mission in the Kingdom of God.) But we live in a day when most pastors and lay leaders (whether men or women) do not know how to heal and free these women, and are, in fact, very much afraid to face such individual spiritual needs at all. Most often when such as these seek help they are shunted into what turns out to be equally binding intellectual and spiritual ideologies (i.e., the pop psychologies, philosophies, or theologies of the day). Or, as an easy way out, their *roles as woman* in the home or in the church rather than their identity as *persons in Christ* are emphasized as the way to wholeness.

Judith's Story

Judy's story, though similar to Renie's in that she had a possessive mother, was quite the opposite from hers insofar as gender balance is concerned. Separated from her prime gender identity, her feminine side, she was in far greater psychological need than Renie had been.

The conscious, analytical, reasoning mind was highly developed in Judy, and she was successful in what had been, until fairly recent date, almost exclusively a man's professional field. She had developed her physical powers to the point of being able to compete with men "on their own turf" in several sports fields as well, and enjoyed pitting her skills and endurance against theirs. The "drive toward power" common to the male was highly developed in her, as was the masculine power to initiate that goes along with it. All this, of course, would have been fine had her feminine side been highly developed as well. But in Judy it simply pointed to an imbalance. Highly developed in the masculine side, she was dwarfed in the feminine. She was out of touch with her heart, the feminine intuitive mind, and totally out of touch with the feminine gender drive. This drive in woman, as pointed out earlier, is the drive to respond to and receive the male. Unless this is stymied, it is natural to woman biologically, physically, and psychologically. Judy had never known this drive.

Because Judy was not in touch with her intuitive side, she was unaware ("unconscious") of her need to forgive her mother. There was a deep-seated anger toward her, though this was completely repressed and denied. But she was very conscious indeed of her need to be released from strong and abnormal compulsions deep within her, those that were directly related to her relationship with her mother and that can accompany a severe symbolic gender imbalance such as Judy knew. The compulsions were lesbian in nature.

She had a history of lesbian activity, and certain women continued to "spark" her, she said. Her need for intimacy was great, and she was, at age thirty-one, utterly unfree to relate to men. "Do I have to live and die with this thing never taken care of in me?" she cried. I assured her she certainly did not have to, and that furthermore there was no such thing, strictly speaking, as a lesbian or homosexual, that there are only those who are separated from some valid though *unaffirmed* part of themselves. I assured her that God would help us find it that very day.

I then asked her what story in *The Broken Image* particularly spoke to her. Here is where the "not being in touch with our own inner self enough to know we haven't forgiven" comes in. She felt she did not quite fit any of the lesbian cases she had read about in *The Broken Image.* As it turned out, hers was a classic example of one category written about in the book, the one where lesbian behavior is primarily connected to a woman's need to be set free from the effects of having an extremely possessive and dominating mother.[2]

Judy's mother was in her late forties when Judy, an only child, was born. When I asked her how her mother was as a feminine role model, she quickly replied: "Oh, I don't think of my mother as a woman." Hearing that statement, I realized she had rejected the femininity of her mother and, in doing so, had somehow rejected her own.

Judy would need to forgive her mother for being a very poor (and as it turned out, even repulsive) feminine role model, and renounce any childhood oaths concerning her before she could go on to accept her own femininity. But her mother had to be forgiven for something else that had been, in Judy's case, the chief culprit behind her lesbian neurosis. From Judy's earliest childhood her mother had systematically and exclusively demanded her daughter's full attention. She was especially keen on cutting her off from contacts with boys and men. The psychological effect of this was to make Judy woman-centered. There was simply no way the gender drive could develop. This had been such an all-pervasive thing in Judy's life that she did not realize how perverse it was or that she needed to forgive her mother for her actions. She felt only guilt for putting half a continent between herself and her mother, and for not continuing to give the attention her mother demanded. The rage she felt toward her mother, though unacknowledged, wrought havoc in the depths of her soul.

Her mother, though she could not say it without profuse apologies for her, was like a vacuum cleaner, always ready to swoop her back up. (It is interesting that she and

Renie should use the same analogy.) Shuddering, she asked me why it affected her so terribly for her mother to say, as she often did, "My life revolves around you. You are my life." She immediately asked the Lord to forgive her for saying such a thing, and started telling me how basically good and well-meaning her mom was. She was amazed to hear me say that rather than apologizing for her mom, she must acknowledge the problem before the Lord and forgive her mother for her actions and words.

Although Judy's main psychological problem was with her mother, and her main healing would come as she forgave her mother and got her identity separated from the maternal source of her being, she would also need to forgive her father. Unlike Renie's father, who came across as a warmly loving and affirming person, and who mitigated at least to some extent the maternal control over her, Judy's father was sort of a "gray blur" in the household, himself totally dominated by his wife. A seemingly totally weak and colorless man, he came through (at least in relation to Judy and her mother) as almost a nonperson. He in no way acted as a buffer between his wife and daughter.

The Prayers and Understanding That Brought Judy's Healing

First I asked Judy if she was willing to repent of and absolutely turn from the lesbian lust. This she was only too willing to do, for, besides wanting to please God, she knew that overt lesbian behavior led only to more misery and did not solve her problem. This prayer and reception of forgiveness opened the way for her psychological healing.

As we talked and prayed, she began to understand her gender confusion and to see how her strong lesbian compulsions had come out of that. The following made the symbolic nature of the problem altogether clear to her. I asked her what chiefly characterized each of the three women who "sparked" her. As she described them, they were very like herself: successful, intellectually keen, and in possession of the power to initiate. But there was one glaring exception. Each of the women were intensely and wonderfully feminine. Here we see the cannibal compulsion again. Judy's strange and compelling drive to hold them and to be held by them was merely a confusing signal of her need to integrate with her own feminine side. She was seeing *in them* her own alienated femininity; indeed, she was projecting her own unrecognized femininity onto them. She would then suffer the compulsive temptation to integrate with it in a physical manner. She was absolutely amazed to see this, and her heart immediately recognized it for the truth.

Besides needing to forgive her mother, Judy needed prayer for the severing of her identity from that of her mother's, along with prayer for a full inner freedom from the bondages the maternal possessiveness and domination had wrought in her. The psychological need in such a case is no small one.

To minister such a healing as this, we invoke the Presence of the Lord, asking for His power and love to come in and enable us to discern, and then to break, the oppressing bondages that have kept the person bound emotionally and spiritually to another. There are different degrees to this problem, of course, but in some it is as though the soul is "possessed" by the soul of the mother. The prayer is much like one of exorcism, only it is for deliverance from the domination of the mother and her inroads into the very spirit and soul of the daughter. One said to me, "My mother has raped my mind." Another, "I can never get away from the presence of my mother, even though I am hundreds of miles from her." It is truly a terrible bondage.

In a case such as this, false guilt will usually need

to be dealt with first. Otherwise the woman may resist (albeit unconsciously) the healing and will rather berate and accuse herself for her problems with her mother. With her is the vague and irrational false guilt of never having been able to please her mother, never being able to meet her expectations, never being able to "love her enough." Pity and sadness for the emptiness in her mother's life will sometimes be paralyzing emotions within the false guilt. In completely disallowing her mother's psychological manipulation she will need to be released from fears that she is being unchristian and unloving. This psychological manipulation is, after all, what she has grown up to think of as "love." She must be assured that it is only after she has accepted her freedom (a full severing of her identity from that of her mother's) that she will be able to love and relate to her mother aright—as a whole, secure person. Until then, there is a part of her which is yet immature, yet under the law of her mother, yet subject to being manipulated. At last assured, she will be prepared to accept her freedom from the subjectivity that keeps her from maturing in some vital part of her personality, if not the whole of it.

In the prayer for such a one's release, I usually ask them to see Jesus with the eyes of their hearts, to see Him on the cross, there taking into Himself the very pain and bondage they are now struggling with, as well as any unforgiveness or sin within their hearts. I ask them to stretch out their hands to Him and see the pain and darkness flow into His outstretched, nail-riven hands as I pray for the severance of their souls from the domination of their mother's. I often, without interrupting the rhythm of the prayer, softly ask them, "What are you seeing with the eyes of your heart?" And it is wonderful what they see as the darkness flows out of them and into Him. Often I will be seeing the same "picture" as the Holy Spirit leads the way.

Then, and I find this to be a very important step, I ask them to picture their mother. Because the Holy Spirit is in control and healing is so powerfully taking place, they will nearly always have a picture of her that is most revealing, one that will enable them to see her objectively for the first time, one that will better enable them to fully forgive her. Then I ask them to look and see if there are any bondages left between them. They will *see* it and *name* it. I then ask them, as though they had scissors in their hands, to cut through the bonds they see. The release that comes with this is often nothing short of phenomenal, and there are times when there are definite emotional and even physical reactions to the release. We will have seen these bonds sometimes as thick diseased umbilical cords, other times as threadlike ropes between the souls of the two, etc. When they are cut, we see a symbolic picture, one that is a true one, of the very deliverance that is taking place.[3]

It was precisely in this way that Judy and I prayed. As she forgave her mother, all the repressed anger and hostility she had been unaware of heretofore began to well up and out of her heart and into our Lord's outstretched hands. From apologizing to Him for even acknowledging the fact that her mother *might* have a problem, she advanced to screaming at her mother, "Mother, every problem I've ever had goes back to you. You have hurt me so badly," etc.

Her heart had believed this all along. But once the situation was faced and admitted, Judy could be delivered from the repressed anger and could fully forgive her mother. Furthermore, she could and did take the fullest responsibility for her own actions, confessing them to the Lord. In prayer to name and cut the bondages between her and her mother, she cried out, "I've got my mother's spirit in me, not Christ's!" She was seeing a gray-brown spirit substance like a sticky cord coming from her mother and winding its way throughout her own body. This was, of course, the way her heart pictured the diseased form of mother-love she had known. I continued to pray for her until she saw this substance flow from her into the crucified body of our Lord. I then prayed for the love and light of Christ to enter in and fill all those spaces where the bondage had been.

After this separation of her identity from that of her mother's, there was yet another very important healing needed. I asked the Lord to enter into her and to find and affirm the beautiful *woman* within. We continued to pray, with laying on of hands, as Jesus touched and healed her in her femininity. There was no way, of course, that she could release faith for this, but we as ministers can learn to.

Last, I prayed for the gift of chastity and celibacy until such time as she married, a prayer that surprised her very much. I have learned to do this, for a repressed gender drive, once released, has a way of making up for lost time. That very weekend she phoned in utter amazement. In a business meeting with a young widower, a Christian man, she experienced for the first time the feminine gender drive. "I've waited a lifetime for this. I sure am glad you prayed for the gift of chastity." This young woman is wonderfully whole today, and her very physical appearance reflects the balance, proper to her as a woman, of the masculine and the feminine within her life.

When Woman Is Bent Toward Her Husband

Renie and Judith were more than willing to forsake any idols they had and to accept the position of identity in Christ and of listening obedience to God. Not all women are. By far the greater number of women need healing at the point of being bent toward their husbands rather than toward mothers and families. These are invariably out of touch with the masculine within themselves, and are in danger of becoming either a nonperson or a very manipulative one. Bent out of the vertical, listening relationship to God where identity is found, they are inclined toward their "idol," and are demanding their identity through him. These women are in great need of prayer for gender balance.

That in Woman Which Works Toward This Bondage

A woman's normal drive to receive from and respond to the male may be perverted into the state of bentness toward her husband, which in turn militates against genuine complementarity in the marriage. Her womanly response, rather than a means to that complementarity, makes an idol of her husband and her marriage. Any icon or sacrament misused and misunderstood, rather than being a vehicle through which the grace of God streams to us, becomes an idol, a terrible object off which we bounce our worst fears and superstitions and are in turn confirmed in them. We take a very good thing and by our misuse of it make it for our minds and hearts a very bad thing indeed. We gain not light and life but darkness and even death through it. So it is with our special qualities as male and female, especially in marriage. In our fallen state these good things are in danger of being held as the highest good, and so idolatry can spring from them. The young men I wrote of earlier, by virtue of their very giftedness *as men,* were seeking affirmation of their masculinity not in God, their highest Good, but in their superior ability to pierce through, shape, and control their outer environment. The young women, by virtue of their giftedness as women and their normal drive to receive and respond to the male, were in danger of attempting to find their affirmation and identity in the love of a man rather than in the love of their Creator.

At the beginning of my adult Christian life I began to understand through my own experience why women had such a difficult time in their realtionships to their husbands. I saw very clearly that woman is bent toward man by reason of the Fall, and *wants* to find her identity in him.

> To the woman he said,
> "I will greatly increase
> your pains in childbearing; with
> pain you will give birth to children;
> *Your desire will be for your husband,*
> and he will rule over you." (Genesis 3:16)

The Lord opened this Scripture to my understanding, and from it I learned to straighten up into the vertical position of finding my identity in Him. In woman's redemption there is healing of this bent position; there is the possibility of obedience to and identity in God, and therefore the discovery of what true Christian submission to one's husband, one's neighbor, one's church is.

To teach, as I do, on incarnational reality and on the work of the Holy Spirit in our lives is to teach on the great subject of Christian freedom. From the very beginning of this ministry I've found women barred from coming into this freedom due to erroneous ideas about what Christian submission is. Some of the neediest women were afraid to obey God, thinking that would mean they were not in submission to their husbands, pastors, or others. Though in great turmoil, they were not free to do the right thing, and were unaware that they (and they alone) were responsible for failing to submit to God.

The problem is not restricted to women. Men can be found whose masculine side is repressed due to mistaken ideas about what constitutes Christian obedience to parents, bosses, and religious leaders. I've seen groups of men and women in religious orders and Christian communities put the real self to death and call that obedience to God—all in the name of humility and Christian submission. A woman, a man, or a group with false notions about what Christian submission is all about cannot listen to God; they cannot effectively obey God. But women are the ones who have been the most harmed.

The Healing of Woman

Although it is not within the purview of this book to go into the social dimensions of women's submission (or women's liberation), we do need to touch upon them, since the psychological hang-ups of so many women are to be found right here. Both, of course, were certainly related to the difficulties Renie, her mother, and her mother-in-law experienced. Their world was boxed in and limited as to notions about the place of woman.

Blocks to our *becoming,* such as those of the women in Richard's family, are often placed there by the church's misunderstanding of both what the place of woman and Christian submission truly are. For example, before recent times the emphasis on a woman's role was so great that it almost entirely precluded the possibility of seeing her as a person. Both Renie and her mother, as well as Richard's mother, had grown up and spent their lives in a culture that emphasized a woman's role while, if it saw her as an individual at all, it saw her only in caricature.

At the height of the extreme teachings on the submission of woman, I began facing one basketcase after another of women who were hurting and desperately seeking help. Many had for the first time found freedom in Christ in the renewal that was spreading throughout great sections of the church. These women were just beginning to blossom when the extreme teachings on submission came flooding in. At the end of seminars on prayer for healing, these tormented women were to be found waiting in long prayer lines for the help they could barely trust was there.

One woman in just such a meeting, after waiting late into the night for prayer, said to me, "If I don't get help tonight, I'm going to kill myself." And she meant it. She had, as it turned out, a severe psychological difficulty with men, one that she did not understand, and her pastor, reminding her that she had a good husband, told her that if she would simply go home and put herself in subjection to him, she'd be fine. First of all, this young wife and mother, all too aware of her husband's fine points and accomplishments, had as yet no sense of a real self or a true self to put in subjection. Never having been affirmed as a woman or as a person by her own father, she as yet was struggling to find a self. She could therefore only misinterpret what her minister was saying, and cease even the weakest attempts to *become,* thinking that she was thereby submitting.

As I prayed with her that night and asked the Lord to bring to the fore any root memory having to do with her fear of men, the deeply submerged memory came up—one that had been utterly repressed. It was of early incest. There had been sexual abuse by her father, a professional man well-respected in the community. Unable to protect and affirm her even as a very young child, he had failed to respect her as a person. Though not abused to the point of rape, she was nonetheless abused genitally. She was treated as an object without love. Not until she came to terms with that, through forgiveness and through acceptance of herself, a self that had been misused and abused by her own father, could she begin to relate positively to her husband and his sexual needs.

Her need was great, and we can readily understand her frustration with herself and with the problem she knew she was causing her husband. But why did her frustration with her pastor's repeated exhortation lead her to seriously contemplate suicide? Her case is, I realize, an extreme though not, unfortunately, a rare case. But why will other less needy women be filled with unaccountable frustration when their pastor or someone else in authority exhorts them or prays for them that they might be good wives or good mothers?

Although a woman suffering in this way will not be able to verbalize it as such, her problem is that her pastor is seeing her in a *class,* not as a person. And he will be, albeit unwittingly, forcing her back into the "fallen position," that of attempting to find her identity in a role or in a creature (her husband or children) rather than in Christ. And she knows at this point the impossibility of that. Her minister would do better to pray like this: "I thank You, Lord, for loving her husband and her children through her." Such would leave the woman's identity intact.

Dorothy Sayers, writing about the need to see ourselves as *persons* first, not as classes, states:

> All categories, if they are insisted upon beyond the immediate purpose which they serve, breed class antagonism and disruption in the state, and that is why they are dangerous. . . . The time has now come to insist more strongly on each woman's—and indeed each man's—requirement as an individual person. . . . To oppose one class perpetually to another—young against old, manual labour against brain-worker, rich against poor, woman against man—is to split the foundations of the state: and if the cleavage runs too deep, there remains no remedy but force and dictatorship.[4]

She goes on to ask: "Are all human beings created to do the same work? No, of course not. . . . We [men and women] are equal in creaturehood—different in functions we were created to perform." But it is pernicious for us to examine "my role as a woman" and "woman's function in modern society" *before* we've examined our roles as *persons*.

Many of us understand the truth of what Dorothy Sayers is saying, and some can even verbalize it quite well. But in most women's hearts a battle—though a quiet one, one that we usually do not understand—continues. Centuries of man's flight from woman, and of erroneous ideas about the place of Christian woman, find quite a foothold in our imaginations and in our deep hearts. We have monitors within that militate on the side of the law, not on the side of grace and freedom. Though we read of the extremely active role women played in the early church, we still cherish the false notion that dying to self means dying to our *power to do and to be* (i.e., our masculine creative will). Therefore, we are always in danger of putting the real self to death. At the very least we risk the imbalance of the masculine and the feminine, both in ourselves and in our relationships with men, and fail to see ourselves as Jesus sees us.

> Perhaps it is no wonder that the women were first at the Cradle and last at the Cross. They had never known a man like this Man—there never has been such another. A prophet and teacher who never nagged at them, never flattered or coaxed or patronised; who never made arch jokes about them, never treated them either as "The women, God help us!" or "The ladies, God bless them!"; who rebuked without querulousness and praised without condescension; who took their questions and arguments seriously; who never mapped out their sphere for them, never urged them to be feminine or jeered at them for being female; who had no axe to grind and no uneasy male dignity to defend; who took them as he found them and was completely unself-conscious. There is no act, no sermon, no parable in the whole Gospel that borrows its pungency from female perversity; nobody could possibly guess

from the words and deeds of Jesus that there was anything "funny" about woman's nature.

But we might easily deduce it from His contemporaries, and from His prophets before Him, and from His Church to this day. Women are not human; nobody shall persuade that they are human; let them say what they like, we will not believe it, though One rose from the dead.[5]

There are of course equally pernicious psychological dangers to be found at the other end of the spectrum—from rigid submission to men to that of extreme feminism. The psychological and spiritual problems of women locked in the confining intellectual and emotional structures of either extreme are equally serious. Even though the character of life formed in each atmosphere differs greatly from the other, both miss freedom. Both bring women into bondage. The woman at either end of the spectrum can succeed in putting the *real self* to death.

It is interesting to me that Dorothy Sayers, one of the first women to graduate from Oxford University, a theologian, novelist, essayist, and author of *Are Women Human?*, was far too brilliant to get involved in feminism as an ideology. She knew the confining nature of such an ideology, of its power to bring about a basic cleavage, not only in a culture but within the human person who espouses it. The gender imbalance within extreme feminists can be a terrifying psychological phenomenon to behold, and those suffering it often cling to it (even in the face of a great deal of psychological pain), calling it wholeness.

A whole woman understands and glories in the fact that the head of man is Christ, and the head of woman is man. She does not usurp authority. (But neither is the man to usurp authority.) But a wise husband, and a wise church leadership, will invite the redeemed, spiritually mature woman to share the headship. David Mains, radio pastor of Chapel of the Air, said it this way, in a conversation over extreme teachings on submission: "The legalist will say: 'The man is responsible.' He is, if he doesn't invite her to share the headship. And what she *is,* a creature of God with gifts, is totally lost. Freedom and submission are both principles in the Scriptures, but *freedom* is uppermost."

Predestination and free will, seemingly opposing principles, are both put forth in the Scriptures, and one does not annihilate the other. God's sovereignty and man's responsibility are both realities. This is also the case with faith and works, and, as we are considering here, with freedom and submission as applied to women's role.

St. Paul writes of freedom and of submission. The Scriptures on woman's submission are one-liners and easy to pull out of context. To understand woman's freedom, a reality much higher and greater and therefore more difficult to define, we must read the whole of Galatians—indeed, the whole of the New Testament. Being careful not to interpret one part of Scripture so it contradicts others, we contrast the texts on submission with those of, for example, Galatians 3:26-28 and Galatians 5. In the Scriptures there are five commands to submit: to God (e.g., James 4:7); to one another (e.g., Ephesians 5:21); to every ordinance of man (e.g., 1 Peter 2:13, 14; Romans 13:1-7); the younger to the elder (e.g., 1 Peter 5:5); wives to husbands (e.g., Ephesians 5:22; Colossians 3:18; 1 Peter 3:1-6).

If we had done with the commands to submit to one another, to every ordinance of man, the younger to the elder, what we have done to the command for wives to submit to their husbands, we'd be, as the body of Christ, in even more trouble than we are in now. The fact is, there are higher laws, higher principles to be obeyed, and these sometimes supersede lower laws or principles. When a political or religious leader, an employer, parent, or husband commands what God forbids or forbids what God commands, we do not submit.

A whole woman knows that there are external authorities to be responded to. But just as in Nazi Germany Dietrich Bonhoffer saw a false usurpation of authority, so a woman must be aware of the more subtle usurpers of an authority that rightfully belongs only to the masculine within *her* and the masculine within *God*. She realizes there are limits to authority, and that higher laws supersede lower ones. Rather than see herself through the eyes of those in the church who mistakenly regard her as a class, and rather than submit herself to a feminist ideology which would again regard her as part of a class, she will look to God for her true identity and the power to transcend her own limitations. All this she will do in order to become the healthy daughter of God and the feminine disciple she was created to be.

There is that in woman which very much needs man to act in the role of headship—just as he needs to ask her to share the headship. Once a man invites the woman to share the headship, both should use their God-given gifts and capacity for leadership. If there is no man to assume headship, then there is something very wrong with the men in the community. There is a crisis in masculinity. To reach a full and balanced leadership capacity, a man needs woman's gifts of leadership and wisdom. And a woman can most be a woman when there is a whole man to respond to *as she leads*.

Woman, then, in order to find wholeness, simply chooses to obey God. She forsakes any "bent" position her gender-drive inclinations have led her to and no longer expects to find her being in and through the man she loves. She understands that failure to accept herself, failure to get through any developmental step due to lack of affirmation as a person or as a woman, will leave her in an immature

spiritual and psychological position, one that almost certainly will lead her to attempt to live through her mate or
someone else. To reach her full maturity in Christ, she must
opt for the whole femininity that complements and com-
pletes her husband's masculinity within the marriage.

When man and woman are reasonably balanced within
themselves, they find that the "sword between the sexes" is
removed. They find they are healed, not in order to dwell
apart with no need for one another, but so that they can
work, love, and worship together—in wholeness.

> There is, hidden or flaunted, a sword between the
> sexes till an entire marriage reconciles them. It is arro-
> gance in us to call frankness, fairness, and chivalry
> "masculine" when we see them in a woman; it is arro-
> gance in them, to describe a man's sensitiveness or tact
> or tenderness as "feminine." But also what poor,
> warped fragments of humanity most mere men and
> mere women must be to make the implications of that
> arrogance plausible. Marriage heals this. Jointly the
> two become fully human. "In the image of God cre-
> ated He *them*." Thus, by a paradox, this carnival of
> sexuality leads us out beyond our sexes.[6]

Notes

Introduction

1. As men have lost the capacity to appropriately touch and call to life (affirm) the feminine within their daughters, the incidence of incest has increased. In one way or another, appropriately or inappropriately, we touch the lives around us. Men either affirm positively the masculine and feminine within their sons and daughters, or by their failure or inability to do so, negate the same.

1: When a Man Walks Alongside Himself

1. Karl Stern, *The Flight from Woman* (New York: Farrar, Straus and Giroux, 1965), p. 39.

2: Man in Crisis: Richard's Story

1. See Leanne Payne, *The Broken Image: Restoring Personal Wholeness Through Healing Prayer* (Westchester, Ill.: Crossway Books, 1981), pp. 76-79 ("Homosexuality Related to Traumatic Experiences in Childhood").

2. *Ibid.*, pp. 46, 47, 66ff.

3. Agnes Sanford, *The Healing Gifts of the Spirit* (Philadelphia: Lippincott, n.d.), pp. 126, 127.

4. To press through the barrier of failure to accept ourselves, far from the formidable thing many perceive it to be, is to embark on an exciting part of our spiritual journey, for to be healed of this failure is to learn to walk in the Spirit. See Payne, *The Broken Image,* pp. 48-58.

5. George Ritchie, *Return from Tomorrow* (Lincoln, Va.: Chosen Books, 1978), pp. 49, 50.

6. Payne, *The Broken Image,* pp. 15-32 ("Lisa's Story").

3: Crises in Masculinity Without Sexual Neuroses

1. W. H. Lewis, ed., *The Letters of C. S. Lewis* (New York: Harcourt Brace Jovanovich, 1975), p. 210.
2. C. S. Lewis, *The Problem of Pain* (New York: Macmillan, 1962), p. 61.
3. For more understanding of prayers of atonement, or penance prayers, examine the scriptural references on atonement. The prayers of atonement in the Old Testament look forward to Christ. The atonement prayers we now pray acknowledge Christ's perfect sacrifice for all sin—past, present, and future. See also Agnes Sanford, *The Healing Light* (St. Paul, Minn.: Macalester, n.d.), Chapter 15 ("For the Healing of the World").
4. Leanne Payne, *Real Presence* (Westchester, Ill.: Crossway Books, 1979), p. 141.

4: What Is Masculinity?

1. Stern, *The Flight from Woman*, p. 39.
2. C. S. Lewis, *That Hideous Strength* (New York: Collier, 1962), p. 315.
3. C. S. Lewis, 'Notes on the Way,' *Time and Tide*, Vol. XXIX (August 14, 1948).
4. *Ibid.* (italics mine).
5. *Ibid.*
6. C. S. Lewis, *The Four Loves* (New York: Harcourt, Brace and Co., 1960), pp. 139, 140.
7. See Payne, *Real Presence*, Chapter 4 for a fuller consideration of this subject.
8. *Ibid.*, Chapter 11.
9. Lewis, *That Hideous Strength*, p. 315.
10. Stern, *The Flight from Woman*, p. 68.
11. *Ibid.*
12. Elisabeth Elliot, *New Covenant*, February 1982.
13. Dr. Elizabeth Moberly, in conversation with Doug Houck, as reported by Robbi Kenney, *Desert Stream Newsletter*, Vol. 2, March/April 1984.
14. Oswald Chambers, *My Utmost for His Highest* (New York: Dodd, Mead and Co., n.d.), June 6.
15. C. S. Lewis, *The Screwtape Letters* (New York: Macmillan, 1962), p. 31.
16. *Ibid.*, p. 39.
17. See Payne, *Real Presence*, p. 89, quoting C. S. Lewis, *Letters to Malcolm: Chiefly on Prayer* (New York: Harcourt, Brace and World, 1963), p. 49.
18. See Payne, *Real Presence*, p. 82, quoting C. S. Lewis, *Letters of C. S. Lewis*, p. 210.

5: The Polarity and Complementarity of the Sexes

1. Stern, *The Flight from Woman*, p. 10.
2. John Gaynor Banks, *The Master and the Disciple* (St. Paul, Minn.: Macalester, n.d.), p. 133.
3. Payne, *The Broken Image*, Chapter 6 ("Listening for the Healing Word").
4. Stern, *The Flight from Woman*, p. 23.
5. *Ibid.*
6. *Ibid.*, p. 21.
7. *Ibid.*, p. 26.
8. *Ibid.*, p. 9.
9. *Ibid.*, pp. 9-11.
10. *Ibid.*, p. 203.

6: Woman in Crisis: The Story of Richard's Wife and Others

1. Stern, *The Flight from Woman*, pp. 38, 39.
2. Payne, *The Broken Image*, pp. 102-106.
3. *Ibid.*, pp. 104-106.
4. Dorothy Sayers, *Are Women Human?* (Grand Rapids, Mich.: Eerdmans, 1971), n.p.
5. *Ibid.*
6. C. S. Lewis, *A Grief Observed* (New York: Bantam, 1961), pp. 57, 58.